THE FOLK-SONGS OF SOUTHERN INDIA

THE FOLK-SONGS OF SOUTHERN INDIA

CHARLES E. GOVER

GYAN

Published by

Gyan Publishing House
5, Ansari Road
Daryaganj, New Delhi-110002
Phone: 011-47034999, 9811692060
E-mail: books@gyanbooks.com

Distribution Network
gyanbooks.com
India, USA, Canada, UK, Australia, France

ISBN : 978-81-212-3383-5 (PB)
First Published, Madras, 1871

2nd Impression 2020

Printed at: Gyan Press, Delhi.

The Folk-Songs of Southern India
Author: Charles E. Gover

THE FOLK-SONGS

OF

SOUTHERN INDIA,

BY

CHARLES E. GOVER,

MEMBER OF THE ROYAL ASIATIC SOCIETY AND OF THE SOCIETY OF ARTS,
FELLOW OF THE ANTHROPOLOGICAL SOCIETY.

MADRAS:
HIGGINBOTHAM AND CO.,
1871.

CONTENTS.

INTRODUCTION.

About half of the songs in the following pages were collected and translated for the Royal Asiatic Society, and were read before that learned body about two years ago. The essays containing them were thought worthy of publication in the journal of the society, but have not yet been issued, as the journal cannot keep pace with the more valuable demands upon its space. A few have also appeared in *The Cornhill Magazine.* Beyond this the present publication is original.

Looking to the mode in which the book has been composed, it may be said that it consists of "Essays written in intervals of business." The portions represented by the papers read before the Royal Asiatic Society were written and their materials collected during occasional sick or other leave, and the pleasant labor thus involved added fresh zest to the enjoyment which a holiday always brings to an overworked Indian official. The remaining portions have been written at times when arduous occupation made change of work a necessity. These facts are not mentioned as a plea *ad misericordiam,* for no author has a right to inflict a bad book on the public on the ground that he is not able to write a good one, but to explain the unequal character of the renderings of the songs and account for certain sudden breaks in the narrative.

Two great objects have been kept in view throughout. First, to exhibit irrefragable evidence of the real feelings of the mass of the people, and thus enable Europeans to see them as they are. Second, to draw public attention to a great body of excellent vernacular literature, in the hope that other persons, far better qualified for the task than myself, will follow the enquiry and publish critical editions and translations of the great ethical works of the Dravidian Augustan period. It is almost impossible now to obtain a printed copy of any early Tamil book that has not been systematically corrupted and mutilated, to meet the views of those whose livelihood depends on the rejection by the public of Dravidian literature and its acceptance of the Puranic legends.

The first principle is of vital importance in connection with a subject that has never been thoroughly examined—the race to which the Dravidian nations belong. Since the learned book by Dr. Caldwell—"Comparative Grammar of the Dravidian languages"—was issued, it has been taken for granted that the Tamils, &c., are a Turanian people. The progress of philological enquiry and the new means of analysis furnished by the great German writers on language have shown the error of this classification. Driven at a very early period into the extreme south, and cut off by vast oceans from intercourse with other peoples, the Dravidian nations have preserved with singular purity the vocabulary they brought with them; and it is probably not extravagant or untrue to say that there is not one true Dravidian root common to tho three great branches, Tamil, Telugu and Canarese, that cannot be clearly shown to be Aryan. As an interesting example both of the true character of the language and the linguistic progress made since the publication of Dr. Caldwell's book, it may be noted that the learned doctor gives an appendix containing a considerable number of Dravidian words which he asserts to be Scythian, and most efficient witnesses to prove the Turanian origin of the language. It is now known that every word in this list is distinctly Aryan, although some of them have representatives in the Finnish group of Turanian tongues—the group which has been most constantly exposed to Aryan influences. The greater portion of them are included in Fick's *Indogermanischen Grundsprache* as Aryan roots, although Fick does not appear to have seen Caldwell's work.

This however is a digression. The songs do not touch the question of roots or derivatives. On another side of the same argument their evidence is decisive. It has always been noted that the true Turanian peoples are inferior to the Aryan in everything connected with the moral nature of man. One recent writer lays it down as a rule that the Turanian peoples display "an utter want of moral elevation." Mr. Farrar, the learned and eloquent author of "Families of Speech," asserts (page 155)—"We may say generally that a large number of them (the Turanian peoples ;—he has previously stated that the exceptions are the Chinese, Finns, Magyars and Turks.) belong to the lowest palœozoic strata of humanity......peoples whom no nation acknowledges as its kinsmen, whose languages, rich in words for all that can be eaten or handled, seem absolutely incapable of expressing the reflex conceptions of the intellect or the higher forms of the consciousness, whose life seems confined to the glorification of the animal wants, with no hope in the future and no pride in the past. They are for the most part peoples without a literature and without a history, and many of them apparently as imperfectible as the Ainos of Jesso or the Veddahs of Ceylon,—peoples whose tongues in some instances have twenty names for murder, but no name for love, no name for gratitude, no name for God."

This is but a fair description of the class to which are said to belong the writers and learners of the songs this book contains. It will be seen that the Dravidian peoples possess one of the noblest literatures, from a moral point of view, the world has seen. Compare with the above, the remarks of the Rev. P. Percival, in his excellent book—"*The land of the Veda.*"—"Perhaps no language combines greater force with equal brevity; and it may be asserted that no human speech is more close and philosophic in its expression as an exponent of the mind....the language, thus specific, gives to the mind a readiness and clearness of conception, whilst its terseness and philosophic idiom afford equal means of lucid utterance." The Rev. W. Taylor, the well known Dravidian scholar, declares of Tamil, the representative Dravidian tongue, —"It is one of the most copious, refined and polished languages spoken by man." And again in his *Catalogue Raisonnée of Oriental MSS.* (vol. I. p. v.) "It is desirable that the polish of the Telugu and Tamil poetry should be better known in Europe: that so competent judges might determine whether the high distinction accorded to Greek and Latin poetry, as if there were nothing like it in the world, is perfectly just." Dr. Caldwell asserts—"It is the only vernacular literature in India which has not been content with imitating the Sanscrit, but has honorably attempted to emulate and outshine it. In one department, at least, that of ethical epigrams, it is generally maintained, and I think must be admitted, that the Sanscrit has been outdone by the Tamil." Three such witnesses, added to the hundred this book contains, suffice to show that, whether as regards literature or morals, the Dravidian people are deserving of and entitled to the honor of omission from the Turanian family.

This is no unimportant matter. Looking to the necessity that the governing race should not be disqualified from performing its noble task by laboring under a complete mistake as to the nationality, aspirations, feelings and errors of the people it rules: seeing that the Dravidian peoples distinctly claim unity of race and origin with the yet more cultivated Sanscrit nation that has settled among them:

knowing that Orientals look as much to points of etiquette, which require in their observer an accurate knowledge of popular social ideas, as to matters of stern fact—would as soon be robbed as lose a title: it is indisputable that there can scarcely be a more serious and interesting question than that which would enquire of the true character and position of the subject nation. All this is over and above that interest and value which is everywhere inherent in all attempts to learn the true life and the inner feelings of any portion of the great human brotherhood.

To show how a simple error in such matters may lead to gigantic mistakes, and because the subject has a close connection with the question under discussion, it will be profitable to examine one feature of the theory started by Dr. Caldwell regarding the South Indian demonolatry. He shows truly enough that the Shanars worship malignant beings, pure devils, and proceeds to note that there is ample proof that the Shanars, and the argument includes the Tamils also, cannot be related to the Sanscrit race. He says—"Every word used in the Tamil country relative to the Brahmanical religions, the names of the gods and the words applicable to their worship, belong to the Sanscrit, the Brahmanical tongue; whilst the names of demons worshipped by the Shanars in the South, the common term for "devil," and the various words used with reference to devil-worship are as uniformly Tamil......The words used with reference to devil-worship being exclusively Tamil, we are obliged to assign to this superstition a high antiquity, and refer its establishment in the arid plains of Tinnevelly and amongst the Travancore jungles and hills, to a period long anterior to the influx of the Brahmans and their civilization of the primitive Tamil tribes."

The most important word thus noted is *Pé* or as Ziegenbalg correctly writes it *Pēy*. It means a devil. The places of worship are called *Pē-Coils*. Another form of the word in Tamil is *penam*, a devil. Now let us follow up this word. It appears in Khond as *Pennu*, the name of the deity. But the object of worship is the sun or the light. Macpherson says—"There is one Supreme Being, self-existing, the source of good, and Creator of the universe." This divinity is sometimes called "the God of Light," by others "the Sun-God, and the sun and the places from which it rises beyond the sea, are the chief seats of his presence." Again Macpherson says—"The Supreme Being and sole Source of Good is styled the God of Light." It is true there are other gods to whom the name *Pennu* is generically given, and even the sun-god takes a pre-name and is known as *Bella Pennu*, literally the "light of the sun." But this, it is clear, does not touch the question, for there are kinds of light which require an adjective for definition. Then subordinate deities arose, to whom, though not representing light, the name was attached. This has happened everywhere. The Sanscrit word "deva" means the deity. But there are Siva Deva, Vishnu Deva, Agni Deva and so on. *Pennu* exactly corresponds with *Deva* and both mean "the light."

But how came *Pennu* or its root form *Pey* to be reduced till it means a devil? Macpherson again gives the answer. He distinctly states that this worship of light is "common to all the tribes." But the Khonds are divided into north, middle, and south confederations. The former has degraded its worship into a demonolatry. The deity exhibits nothing but "pure malevolence towards man, and they believe that while no observances or course of conduct can change her malignant aspect into benignity, her malevolence may still be placed in partial or complete abeyance by the sacrifice of human life, which she has expressly ordained." He describes the rites of this horrid superstition, and they are the exact counterpart of the Shanar devilry, where, by the way, the male god has also been changed into a female devil. The Khonds of the middle region have maintained the true and earlier doctrine. Macpherson says of their deities, the same as those worshipped in the north—"No malevolence towards mankind is ascribed to them. On the contrary they are merciful and benign towards those who observe their ordinances and discharge their rites. Instead of delighting in cruel offerings, they abhor the inhuman ritual of the northern, southern and western districts; and they would resent with detestation any semblance of participation in it by their worshippers."

This teaches us two things. First, that demonolatry may surround deities that were originally good, —human passions and fears may change a good into an evil spirit. Second, that the true meaning of the word *Pey* or *Pennu* is not "devil" but "light."

But Dr. Caldwell asserts that the word is neither Sanscrit nor related to Sanscrit. This is a strange error. Before Caldwell wrote, it had been frequently noted that the Dravidian *Pe* or *Pey* is identical with the root of the Sanscrit *pi-sacha,* meaning a devil, a malevolent being. The words are interchangeable. There is no reason to suppose that the Tamil word is derived from Sanscrit or vice versa, yet the roots are identical. But Sanscrit authorities ascribe *pisacha* to a root *pis,* to adorn, and this, as given by Benfey, has the parallel form *pimśa* from the root *pims* to shine. This exact coincidence in both Dravidian and Sanscrit forms proves their identity beyond a doubt. The Sanscrit forms just quoted probably belong to the great cluster of important roots that has its centre in *Bhā,* to shine. Thus the Tamil *Pēy* and the Khond *Pennu* find their exact equivalents in the Greek *phaō* and *phainō,* from the root *pha.* The same derivative appears in the gods *Phanos* and *Phaethon.*

But the Dravidian tongues do not need these foreign analogies to show that *pey,* a devil, comes from a root meaning light. In Madi *pey-al,* in Rutluk *piy-al,* in Madia *biy-ar,* in Tamil *pag-al,* in Tuluva *pag-il,* all mean day, the light time. *Al* and *il* are merely substantive terminations. In ancient Tamil *pi-rei* was the moon, and in modern *vey-il* is the sunlight. In another dialect *pēymoro* is the light. A hundred other examples might be given, proving beyond doubt that the Tamil *pey* originally meant *the bright one,* that is, the deity. As some Khond tribes made *Pennu* the god of light a devil, so some of the Tamils, when cut off from the better teaching of the fathers of their race, degenerated in their worship and degraded their deity to match their superstition.

It has always been easy to change a god into a devil. The last word used is an illustration, for *devil* is a clear derivative from *deva,* and is closely related to "deity?" Opposing nations have ever called the gods of their adversaries devils. But enemies are not needed for this change. Ignorant sinful man must ever look upon God as a being to be propitiated rather than loved, and when such propitiation becomes an instrument in the hands of ignorant and poor but greedy priests, it pays well to make the deity as dreadful as possible, that offerings may be the more readily made to appease it. Out of Hinduism came the devilry of Sakti. Kali the protector and avenger is now Durga the devil.

The name of the devil-god of Tinnevelly, when thus carefully examined, proves the exact opposite of what Dr. Caldwell would learn from it. He asserts—"of elementary worship there is no trace whatever in the......usages of any portion of the Tamil people." The word shows, in reality, that the demonolatry is corrupted from an early worship of the element light. In the Khond country all the elements are worshipped. Caldwell asserts that the Tamils are not related to the Aryan race, and adduces the name and worship of dovils as evidence. The name proves that the deity is Aryan, and there is every reason to believe the worship to be but one example of a process that happened in many Aryan races. Caldwell employs the facts under notice to prove the Turanian origin of the people. Their evidence is entirely on the other side, though by no means conclusive either way.

The composers, teachers and, generally, the singers of the songs belong to a distinct class in Hindu society. The better castes will seldom sing, although most liberal in their treatment of the professional singers. Women will sing to their children, boys will in their lightness of heart hum the more popular melodies both in the street and at home, and there are merry housewives who are fond of exercising their sweet voices while performing their ordinary domestic duties. As a rule, however, and invariably in public, the singers belong to the religious mendicant fraternities; who make their chants subservient to their fortunes, and sing for the scanty livelihood which falls to the beggar's lot in a land where beggars are plentiful as blackberries in Epping Forest.

The greater part of the singers now-a-days belong to the anomalous class called *nattuvan*, the sons of dancing girls, knowing nothing of their fathers and, therefore, of the caste to which they should belong. Formerly they were rigorously shut out of the Hindu body politic, yet, as their mothers, they were not despised or treated as outcastes. They were the property of the God, bound to his service, entitled to a share in his offerings. They grew up as musicians, as lighters of lamps, as stewards and general servants in the pagodas. In modern times the English law has made a vast difference in their condition. If the mother be well-to-do and can give her son a good education, she tacks the caste title "Moodelliar" after his name and sends him away from the place of his birth to a district where his antecedents are not known. In his new position none can deny that he is a Vellala. If he become rich none would wish to refuse him the privilege. Choosing the daughter of some poor Vellala who finds it prudent to ask no questions, he marries into his assumed caste. The issue of the marriage are as good Vellalas as those who came in the train of Agastya. In this way the sons of the temple women are constantly absorbed.

Formerly such things could not be done. The *nattuvan* found himself an outsider, civilly treated it is true, but yet without a privilege and almost without a right. Their numbers were constantly increased. Wives were always ready to their hands in the female offspring of the dancing girls that were not well favored enough to follow the profession of their mothers. Thus the race was perpetually recruited. Things might have gone badly both for them and the caste people had not a door been open for their entrance into decent life. There has always existed a class of devotees named *dasas* or slaves to the deity. A man in deep trouble vowed that if God should spare him he would devote himself to God's service. Sick men in fear of death vowed themselves to the life of a dasa if they but recovered. Women longing for children vowed their first-born to the deity that would give them issue. Rebels in imminent danger of a horrible death fled to the temple to find sanctuary in the life of a slave. Brahmans who had infringed the laws of their caste found a safe haven and an accustomed life in the same state.

No questions of caste entered into the matter. Any man might become a *dasa,* and any woman might enter the ranks of the *dasi.* The dasa's duty was to serve God at all hazards, at all loss. The Sanyassi was a dasa, the Yogi was a dasa, but the class included many who had small claim to sanctity. They must have no worldly occupation but begging, they could have no home but the forest or the pyalls of houses in the villages. Their service was, first of all, poverty; secondly, singing; thirdly, forgetfulness of caste. Their reward lay in human honor and the certainty of a living. None dared to despise the "slave of God," none could refuse him a handful of rice or a couple of oppams or chupatties. At weddings and feasts, at fasts and funerals, at sowing and harvest, at full moon and sankranti (the passing of the equator as the sun changed its tropic,) the dasa must be invited, listened to, and rewarded. At weddings, he must sing of Krishna; at burnings, of Yama; before maidens, of Kama; before men, of Rama. As he begs he sings of right and duty; when he hears the clink of copper in his shell, of benevolence and charity.

Here then was the centre to which the nattuvan converged, where he stood shoulder to shoulder with Brahmans, Vellalas and Chetties. If he loved liberty he left wife and child to live as an ascetic. If he loved ease he set up as poojari or director of some wayside shrine to Hanuman, Vighnēswara, or Krishna. If he loved profit he learned to read the Puranas and sometimes even the Vedas, and came before the world as a pundit skilled in logic and perfect in ritual and sacrifice. In either case he became the bard of his neighbourhood, emphatically "the singer." If such men be worshippers of Vishnu they are called Satani or Chatali, and, in the Tamil country, Tadan. If they adore Siva they are known as Pandarams; while if they belong to the uncompromising reformers known as Vira Saivas or Lingayets they receive the title of Jangams.

There can be few more pleasant scenes than when, in the cool of the evening, the dasa enters some quiet country village to find and earn his food and quarters for the night. Marching straight to the mantapam or many-pillared porch of the pagoda he squats on the elevated basement, tunes his vina, places before him his huge begging shell. The villagers are just returning from the fields, weary with their labors, anxious for some sober excitement. The word is quickly passed round that the singer has come, and men, women and children turn their steps towards the mantapam. There they sit on the ground before the bard and wait his pleasure. He begins by trolling out some praise to Krishna, Vishnu or Pillaiyarswami. Then he starts with a *pada* or short song such as those with which this book commences. There is chorus to every verse. If the song be well known, before the bard has finished the long-drawn-out note with which he ends his verse, the villagers have taken up their part and the loud chorus swells on the evening breeze. If the song be new they soon learn the chorus, and every fresh verse bears a louder and louder refrain. Then the shell is carried round and pice are showered into it. When darkness closes in, the headman of the village invites the singer to his house, gives him a full meal and then leaves him with mat, vina and shell to sleep on the pyall. In busy towns the singer squats by the roadside and soon collects a crowd to hear his song. The chorus here is less frequently heard. The people cannot stay, their children are at home, they hear a little and then pass on.

The contents of the following pages will give samples of almost every kind of songs that thus catch the public ear and dwell in the national heart. The only exceptions of which I am aware are the episodes of the great epics and the erotic chapters which I dare not translate. Neither belong to our subject, for both are purely Brahmanic, entirely foreign to the Dravidian literature and mind. The word "samples" is advisedly used. There is a great mass of noble writing ready to hand in Tamil and Telugu folk literature, especially in the former. Total neglect has fallen upon it. Overborne by Brahmanic legend, hated by the

Brahmans, it has not had a chance of obtaining the notice it so much deserves. The people cling to their songs still, and in every pyall-school the pupils learn the strains of Tiruvalluva, Auveiyar, Kapila, Pattunatta and the other early writers.

To raise these books in public estimation, to exhibit the true products of the Dravidian mind, would be a task worthy of the ripest scholar and the most enlightened government. I would especially draw attention to the eighteen books that are said to have received the sanction of the Madura College, and are among the oldest specimens of Dravidian literature. Any student of Dravidian writings would be able to add a score of equally valuable books. If these were carefully edited they would form a body of Dravidian classics of the highest value. If the syndicate of the university could be persuaded to lend themselves to a task so noble, they could with ease ensure that publication should meet with a demand sufficiently extensive to pay for the cost of editing. In the Rev. P. Percival, Madras, has a scholar of remarkable powers who yet has vigor and leisure enough to accomplish a task so great.

It may not be considered a digression to protest against the Christian mutilation to which the Tamil classics are now liable, an offence not inferior in demerit to that Brahmanic mutilation which has been so frequently referred to in the text. A school of Christians has arisen so forgetful of what is due to the great laws of right as to be desirous of compelling a Tamil author to run in a Christian groove. They object to that most praise-worthy act by which the author of a Dravidian book dedicates his book to the god he serves. Men who learnt Juvenal at college and who send their sons to England to become learned in all the wisdom and vice of Greece and Rome: who are proud when their sons gain prizes for proficiency in Ovid or Terence: are so unconscious of the puerility and inconsistency of their acts as to think it a sin to read and explain the humble dedication of his work to his god by some poor Hindu. Would to God that Christians were equally mindful of the duties they owe their Maker! A learned and estimable missionary has been publicly condemned because he would faithfully translate a noble poem without a really impure thought in it, and was, therefore, compelled to commit the awful crime of likening a woman's bosom to a pomegranate. Aye, condemned by men who read the song of Solomon in their families and from their pulpits.

A mere conventionality has tabooed all verbal reference to matters that enter into the life of every sentient being. It is perhaps well that it should be so, but nothing is more absurd than to carry such conventionalities into our estimation of foreign literatures, where such rules are unknown. This principle is always borne in mind with regard to the European classics, but is forgotten when Indian classics are in question. A large portion of modern Dravidian literature carries freedom into license, but of such books we need know nothing. In the early literature there is little that so sins, and it is unpardonable that Christians, who ought to be above fashionable conventionalities and free from any suspicion of wrong-doing, should deliberately mangle a fine work of art because it will not fit modern English proprieties or modern narrow-minds.

At the risk of unduly extending this preface, it will be well to prove this point by quoting the following from the "Classified Catalogue of Tamil printed books" by that laborious, energetic and wandering genius, Dr. Murdoch, whom to know is to respect.

"The Vedas have never been translated into Tamil; the writings of Auvaiyar, Tiruvalluvar, and other poets, form the real moral and religious code. They are taught in every native school, and their *dicta* are received as infallible truth. The bulk of the verses are unobjectionable; some of them are of great beauty and excellence. There are, however, intermingled passages, inculcating idolatry and superstition of various kinds. The following may be quoted as specimens from the edition of the Tamil Minor Poets, printed at the Public Instruction Press for use in Government Schools:—

Invocations.—"Milk, sweet honey, syrup, and grain, these four mixed together, to thee will I give. Do thou O majestic, noble, elephant-faced one, thou holy jewel, grant me the three kinds of Tamil common in the world."—p. 28.

"Let us ornament our heads with the wonderful flower, the foot of the five-handed glorious one, who is the mystic syllable, Om."—p. 14.

Worship of Vishnu.—"Serve Vishnu."—p. 6.

Worship of Siva.—"To those who medidate on Si-va-ya-na-ma, there will be no suffering at any time: this is the way of overcoming the decree of destiny; this is true wisdom; but fate will be the cause of all other occurrences to men."—p. 31.

Rubbing of Sacred Ashes.—"The forehead without sacred ashes is void of beauty."—p. 31.

Pantheism.—"He will not make any distinction saying, 'This is good and this is bad,' 'I did this and he did that,' 'This is not and this is;' but in his state of perfection, it will be true of him that 'he himself is that,'" (meaning God.) —p. 36.

Fatalism and Transmigration.—"Each must enjoy the fruits of his actions done in former births according to what Brahma has written (on the forehead.) Oh king, what shall we do to those who are angry with us? Though the whole town together be opposed to it, will destiny be frustrated?"—p. 34.

Although in these days of religious indifference, the worship of "Jehovah, Jove, or Lord," may be regarded with equal eye, every right-minded Christian will shudder at countenancing in the slightest degree the crime of high treason against the God of heaven. The British Government rightly puts down, with a strong hand, rebellion against itself; it forbids the teaching in its schools of the blessed words, "Believe in the Lord Jesus Christ, and thou shalt be saved;" yet in Government school-books youths are taught to worship the gods of the Hindu pantheon, and to believe that their foreheads are void of beauty unless they bear the mark of rebellion against their Creator."

In the extracts given by Dr. Murdoch, we have the worst he could find, and there is not one that is in the slightest degree objectionable, remembering that we read Tamil authors. There is not a word that can be compared with the impropriety of the "Christian" paragraph with which Dr. Murdoch closes. Such forgetfulness of charity is always next door to misrepresentation. He would have it that, because Hindu boys are required in school to read a Hindu book embodying certain phrases, they are "taught to believe that their fore-heads are devoid of beauty unless they bear the mark of rebellion against Christ." This is just as true as a similar assertion that, because in school we read the Metamorphoses of Ovid, we are thereby taught to believe that Proteus or Jove is the true God, and that their disguises are true incarnations of the deity.

I candidly profess that I can see no difference in guilt or folly between those who would modify Sivavakyer in a Christian direction, and those who would make him speak Puranism. There is no better way of perpetuating evil, or what is deemed evil, than to treat it evilly, and the expurgated and improved editions of some missionaries only lead Hindu enquirers to rush to the genuine book and seek for the suppressed passages. Every man of ordinary experience knows that the very best mode of advertising a thing, be it good or bad, is to cause it to be suppressed. Thus "improved" editions seldom gain their end.

It was at first intended to issue with this book the vernacular originals of certain of the songs. This design has been abandoned for the following reasons :

1st.—It was deemed of primary importance to make the selection of songs as wide as possible, so as to cover the greater part of the Dravidian peoples. This made it necessary to occupy the whole book with English renderings. Not only so, but the book is now considerably larger than was at first intended and announced.

2nd.—So many languages are represented that few readers would be able to follow more than a small portion of the originals, and the rest would be so much waste paper.

3rd.—It is hoped that an attempt will be made to issue the genuine critical editions referred to on page xx., and it will be better in every way to have complete series of the songs and poems of which specimens only have been given in this book, than to allow an important literature to continue represented by a few examples.

It remains to speak of the great assistance with which I have been favored. No mention is made in the text of the help to which I am so much indebted with regard to the Canarese songs. It was intended to speak in this place of the kindness which has been so bountifully exhibited in the collection and translation of the songs generally; but, while the book was passing through the press, a discussion arose in the English press regarding the best mode of expressing the obligations due to friendly aid in literary work. It was there decided that such obligation should be acknowledged in the text where it is exhibited. From the Badaga songs onwards, the help afforded me has been gratefully acknowledged. I regret that one amendment is necessary, with regard to the Coorg songs and explanatory text. I have spoken strongly and justly of Mr. Richter's kindness, but now learn (from an article and letter in the *Madras Times*) that Mr. Richter had himself employed the language of an eminent missionary, Dr. Moegling, to whom therefore my first thanks are due. Dr. Moegling's book contains the whole of the explanatory prose inserted as quoted from Richter's Manual, but does not contain a line of any of the songs. The unfortunate mistake made by Mr. Richter will not invalidate any one of the many services he has rendered to Coorg.

Of the Canarese songs it is necessary to speak at greater length. I owe the originals to the kindness of two excellent and able missionaries, the Revs. A. J. O. Lyle and S. Dalzell. They followed in the footsteps of the Revs. T. Hodson and J. Stephenson, and thus a considerable body of the Dasarapadas has been collected. The two gentlemen first named gave me literal translations of most of the songs, and these I rendered as they now appear. I am not aware that they have ever before been translated into English, except that some five or six, put into metre by the Rev. Messrs. Stephenson and Greenwood, appeared in a magazine now extinct, the "*Harvest Field.*" After the first paper for the Royal Asiatic Society was sent home, I learnt through Mr. Eggeling, the secretary of the society, that Dr. Moegling had previously published the text and a German translation of many of the songs in Vols. 14 and 18 of the Journal of the German Oriental Society. Before this I had come across a rare Canarese text of twenty-four songs lithographed by Dr. Moegling. It is a pleasure to ascribe to Dr. Moegling the credit of having first drawn attention to this very interesting literature, and to follow in his footsteps. Lest however he should be held responsible for such errors as may have crept into these pages, it is necessary to state that the only portion of Dr. Moegling's labors that has been before me is the lithographed Canarese text above referred to, and this not till the greater part of my renderings were complete.

For the text of the Malayalam songs I am indebted to my brother, A. G. Gover, Esq., Barrister-at-Law, who was kind enough to make diligent search at my request. Some of the Tamil songs, and much aid throughout, I owe to a young native friend, Mr. T. Davaraju Pillai, B. A., to whom my warm thanks are due.

It would be wrong to conclude without publicly and gratefully acknowledging how much of whatever merit this book may possess is owing to the kind encouragement of the Lord Napier, K.T., who has taken the greatest interest in the work from its commencement, and whose suggestions and criticism have been of material benefit. But for the liberal subscriptions of His Lordship and of the Madras Government, the book would not have been published, nor would the collection of songs have been so complete. The Madras Government has shown of recent years a most earnest desire to obtain and publish all available information concerning the condition and wants of the great people it rules, and if this work should throw any light on so important a subject the pleasant labor of its composition will not have been in vain.

Nor must I omit to mention the generous aid of Colonel Meade, the Chief Commissioner of Mysore, and of Sir Seymour Fitzgerald, the Governor of Bombay. Both gentlemen have, on the part of their respective governments, done all that lay in their power to forward an enquiry which cannot fail to be interesting and may be productive of very important results.

November 15*th*, 1871.

THE FOLK SONGS

OF

SOUTHERN INDIA.

It has often been said that there is no better way of discovering the real feelings and ideas of a people than that afforded by the songs that pass from lip to lip in their streets and markets. None know from whence they come. Verses are added to or subtracted from them as new ideas come in or old ones pass away. Thus they keep up to date, as it were, the expression of those inner feelings which never rise to the surface of a set literature, but are in reality the very essence of popular belief. Their satire is often sharp, and never fears to attack shams, however venerable they may be. Such satire is often the only means left to the illiterate and obscure of showing that the priestcraft, the outer polish, the grosser abuses as well as the showier fabrics, which to outsiders seem to be the life of the nation, are in no sense the life or even a portion of the life of the millions who in reality form the mass of the nation, but who are far too often utterly forgotten by those who judge a people by its upper ten thousand. A lengthened residence in India has shown that the Dravidians or Hindus of Southern

India, and probably all others, are not what ordinary descriptions of Hinduism would make them out to be. With the exception of a few monographs like Hunter's Rural Annals, and occasional descriptions of village life, almost all books that have come before the public proceed upon the assumption that, as are the Brahmans, so are the Hindus. They are filled with descriptions of Brahman ceremonial. They comprehend only Brahman literature. The vices and the virtues of the priesthood are ascribed to the nation as a whole. There seldom seems to dawn upon the mind a single suspicion that perhaps so exclusive a caste, so jealous of contact with the impure masses around, so determined to keep to itself all the religious books, so pertinacious in maintaining its own essential superiority, is not a fair representative of the masses it despises, and with whom it will have no dealings. As a matter of fact the Brahmans are as different from *the people* in social habit, religious practice, and mode of thought, as the Greek philosophers from the vulgar crowd in Thessaly or Sicily, who plodded in their fields sublimely indifferent to the wrangles of Epicurean and Stoic, Peripatetic and Platonist.

Even in religious Hinduism the same truth holds good. The modern representative Brahman scorns the service of the temples, and looks upon the actual priests as a lower caste. In hundreds of pagodas the poojari is not a Brahman at all; and the churchwardens, under the system recently introduced by the Indian Government, are seldom Brahmans, even in the larger and more sacred shrines. While the lower castes flock to the temple festivals, the Brahman discourses in his house upon the Vedanta, or criticizes the doctrines of Sancaracharya, Ramanuja and Madhvacharya—systems in which idolatry and polytheism have as small a share as in the works of Berkely, Mill, or Spinosa. Even the purohita, formerly the highest dignitary in the Aryan economy, is now degraded into an inferior,—one who must minister to the ignorance and superstition of the crowd.

The Brahmans of Southern India are divided into three great sects—those who believe that there is but one soul, in short, that everything is God, (adwaita)—those who believe that there are two souls, God and Man, (dwaita)—and those who take a medium course and believe that there is but one soul, which in man and created things is somewhat different from the divine soul, (visishta adwaita). To those who are not Brahmans these philosophical distinctions are almost unknown, and men worship a being to whom they give the puranic names of Vishnu and Siva, Krishna and Hanuman. While so many names are given and acknowledged by every Hindu, as if each referred to a separate deity, each person acknowledges but one as his own God and ascribes to him all the attributes of the Godhead.

It will be seen, however, that while the philosophy of the schools is unknown to the crowd, the strong tendency of the popular mind is towards monotheism of a character not unlike that of the Visishta Adwaita school. Vishnu and Siva are, according to books, members of a triad of equal Gods, but in popular theology the worshipper of either scorns the others. One of the songs that follow condemns as utterly foolish the man who honors Siva when his professed God is Vishnu. In social life and act the worshipper of Vishnu acknowledges but one god. He speaks of Vishnu as if there were no other god. So with the devotee of Siva, even in a greater degree. He transposes the name into the neuter, Sivam ; and expresses thus his belief that his deity is the one great essence, without sex or corporeal shape.

This distinction has been abundantly and accurately explained by many great writers. Yet the truth has never come home to the European mind, because, as such works went through the press, they were accompanied, and much more than out-numbered, by other books on India—chiefly written by missionaries. The latter dilated upon the enormities of vulgar Hinduism, its millions of deities, the obscenities, quarrels, defeats, and victories of the gods themselves. Clubbing these together under the shade of the old proverb—"as are their gods so are the people"—these authors have ascribed utter abominations to the mass of the people, until it has become the general idea that all under the ranks of the higher Brahmans is one seething mass of impurity, polytheism, and the grossest superstition. Far be it from me to reflect upon the self-denying and able men who have done so much to renovate India. The greater the earnestness with which such men as

Ward, Arthur, Heber, Ziegenbalg, Duff and a host of worthy compeers, applied themselves to their great work, the more were they driven to abhor the religious system that stood in their way, that is, the puranic ritual of the pagodas. They naturally looked to the priests and temples as representing Hinduism. The temple Brahmans, excluded from the society of their more intelligent brethren, have undoubtedly given ample cause for every reproach. The traditions of the gods as repeated in the temples are, to the present day, too often hideous beyond conception. The literature floated by the same class is obscenity itself. The gods are viler than devils elsewhere.

But it has not been noticed how great is the gulf between even the low class Brahmans and the higher members of the Sudra caste. The Sudra hears these stories in the temples, receives them without a blush and passes them on to his sons; but, out of the temple, he is another man. The Brahman cannot come to his house except to perform certain religious ceremonials, may not eat with him, may not even touch him, dares not speak to the women who are moulding the next generation, does not even see him again until he goes to some festival, which may not come for another month. Meanwhile the Sudra lives, works, rules his house, performs his daily devotions. He sees wherever he goes, and in whatever he does, that truth and chastity, honesty and industry, and all those other virtues that the gods despise, are the keys of peace and happiness. He knows that obscenity at home will only bring ruin, and keeps his wife almost under lock and key. He soon learns that, however it may be among the gods, industry and skill are better things than idleness and begging. He is as sure as he is of his life that he cannot do business, cannot provide for his family, unless he keep his promise and meet his bond. If such be the case, there can be no hesitation in his choice—the gods perhaps have a different rule of life, because they are gods; but that is their look-out. As for him he will listen to and applaud the amorous tricks of a Krishna and the thefts of other divinities, but they must not shape his life.

But these Vaisyas and Sudras form the people. The Brahmans, all told, are not more than a fraction of the population. Even in Madura, a stronghold of the faith, they are but one to fifty of the other castes. In Northern India they are much more numerous, but in the North-west Provinces they are only one in seven. Everywhere it is the other castes that form the working population, and it is they that have the right to be considered the people of India. Close observation for several years, and the extended friendship with Hindus with which I have been honored, have long shown that in all matters of daily life the popular Hinduism of the priests is not found among the lower castes. If such an illustration may be permitted it might be said that modern Hindu life in Southern India much resembles that of Europe just before the Reformation. Instead of ascendancy on the side of the priest and deference on the part of the people, there was antagonism, not only in act but much more in thought and word. The priests were necessary evils, not to be got rid of, but existing as the mark of satire, and a vast proof that religion and morals need not coincide. Church festivities became fairs rather than times of worship, and even the very churches were given over to "Lords of Misrule;" while the most sacred mysteries of religion were made the means of murder and the sport of those who were most bound to revere them. Yet everywhere there was the feeling that, after all, the church was something that at times ought to be dreaded. A man might live scorning the priests, but he dared not die without absolution. He might break every commandment when it suited him, but he must be prepared for penance or pilgrimage when his sins made him uncomfortable. Such is really popular Hinduism now, and so has it been for many generations past.

It will be said that such a state of things could not continue; that the Reformation was the necessary result of the time of Erasmus; and that some such movement must have happened in India had the above description been true. Precisely, and just such a revolution, modified by nation and locality, has taken place; except that it has worked itself out so silently that few Europeans have been aware of its existence. Religious Hinduism in Southern India is now a thing of sects, each under its own guru. It requires the acuteness and learning of a Colebrooke to describe the bearings and specialities of each sect. Every Hindu below the

Brahman caste chooses his sect, distinguished by certain marks and signs. He promises unhesitating obedience to the guru, who is seldom a Brahman, and gives him divine honors. Every year he pays a certain proportion of his income for the maintenance of his guru, and the support of the sect. Occasionally the guru travels in great state through the districts which contain the most of his adherents. Everywhere he collects his dues, receives offerings and gifts, teaches the peculiar doctrines of the sect, initiates new members and, in short, performs in an Indian fashion the functions of a Pope. Very little is known of the inner workings of these sects, but as a general rule it may be accepted as a fact that while they do not absolutely reject the ordinary puranic system—that is, the Brahmanic traditional system described above—their general tendency is to import the results of the philosophical systems of the higher Brahmans, and present a scheme, more moral than religious, in which idolatry is unknown, and the divinity is always spoken of as the great soul of the universe, one and indivisible. There has been no open breach between the old and the new systems, and few members of a sect will condemn the most flagrant instances of immorality exhibited in the temples. Nor will they refuse to join in the ordinary temple services. The excuse always given is that these things are fit for the vulgar crowd, and it is not right to depart from the customs of their sires. This silent revolution has been, as far as can now be seen, altogether independent of European influence and agency. In fact, by giving to the people a more refined system of religious thought, it has greatly tended to hinder the spread of Christianity. It had begun long before the rise of the British power.

All this points to the fact, with which we started, that the people of India are not accurately described from Brahman sources ; and that in thought and habit they are, in a marked sense, different from the sacred caste. This has often been noticed ; but there has always been a great lack of material for proving it to those who have not lived in India or, having lived there, took their knowledge from Brahmans. It is necessary that the proof should be really popular and purely indigenous. The dramas published by the Rev. J. Long have done much to reveal local feeling in Bengal, but Madras has not been so fortunate as to possess an enquirer of like character. The following pages contain the result of an attempt to fathom the real feelings of the masses of the people, by gathering and collecting the folk songs of each family of the great Dravidian nation. It has been the pleasant labor of years to make this collection—in the plains where dwell the Tamil and Telugu peoples : on the Mysore plateau, the home of Canarese : among the hills and valleys of the Neilgherries and the Western Ghauts, sheltering the stalwart tribes of Coorg and the humble Badagas of Ootacamund : along the narrow strip of low-lying coast that parts the sea from the Western Ghauts and gives a home to the Malayalim tongue.

It would be unwise to describe the songs beforehand,

when the reader will find them for himself in the pages that follow. It is, however, permitted to point out the more salient features that mark them all. First and foremost we see deep aversion to the lower Brahmanic system, and a vigorous clinging to the love and goodness of the deity. I say *the* deity, for there is no trace of a plurality of gods. Vishnu, Purandala Vithala, Brahma, Yama may be named, yet they are but epithets for the one God and his minister, death. The temple stories find no place here except, now and then, like Jannes and Jambres in the New Testament epistle, as references to a popular legend, legend really.

No one can fail to be struck with the sadness that prevails. The world and every soul in it are so sinful, so full of all evil, that man should give up all to save his life; and even then can hardly hope to succeed. "How to cross the sea of sin?" becomes the great question. Its current is so strong, its waves so high, its hidden rocks so many, that none but a strong swimmer can dare to hope to reach the other side. Even he is so battered by storm and rock, so exhausted by the contest or worn by exertion, that when he seems able to touch the shore his strength may fail, his heart grow weak, and he sink back into the roaring tide. If things be so with the vigorous manful few, how can the feeble trembling many ever hope to see the golden feet of the god whose help they crave? It is inexpressibly saddening again and again to note such songs as these, and know that they represent the inmost feelings of the better part of a great nation.

It is not hard to find the cause of so much sorrow. To the great mass of the nation there is positively no way open towards religious peace, except in that hardest of all courses—abstract faith in an abstract deity. Virtue is its own reward, it is true; but sin has its pleasures as well, and they are near. Who knows what is virtue's reward in a Hindu country? Brahmanism has little hold of the national mind in Dravida. The Brahmans are foreigners, their doctrines or rather legends, as taught in the temples, are repulsive or else vicious, and no man can rest a troubled heart in them. The philosophical systems of the thoughtful Brahmans are jealously kept from the masses. What then have they?

Many of the songs would seem to show that the crowd lean tenderly towards the Buddhist doctrines of absorption and annihilation. "It is better to die than live," —better to die and never again know life, than to run the risk of a new birth that may only produce fresh sorrow, increased pain, and plunge the soul into another series of births each worse than the last. If to live is but to suffer such fears, doubts, and pangs as man has, it is better not to live,—better to forfeit the possibility of one day entering into the higher life, than to meet the certainty of what seems a never-ending cycle of forfeitures and penalties induced by that omnipresent sin which not one out of a million can successfully resist. But future nothingness, though better than constant pain, is not a hopeful prospect. It is an escape to be grateful for, not a pleasure to be proud of. To be merely free from pain is but a very low goal for the human soul to aspire to, and cannot give that zest and glory to life which are required to make a man joyous while he suffers, peaceful when surrounded by anxieties, triumphant when he dies. He who would live righteously in this present life is driven back on every side. No repentance opens his way to pardon. A pardon bought by offerings to despised priests and immoral shrines will give no peace when Death draws nigh. The sorrowing man is too ignorant to fathom the philosophy of the schools, and too old to begin to learn.

The songs divide into several classes. 1st, Moral songs, dealing with the subjects described in the last para. 2nd, Proverbial philosophy. This is a very large class. 3rd, Songs representing the Adwaita system, filled with high morality but strongly pantheistic, and hence exhibiting the most curious paradoxes regarding human conduct. 4th, Ancient Tamil songs of the period when Dravidianism and Brahmanism were struggling for the mastery—when men like Tiruvalluva and Sivavakyer used their tongues and pens in favor of deism and against the ceremonial polytheism of the Brahmans,—when the best men poured out what are distinctly called "songs of sorrow," and were very Jeremiahs in weeping over the corruptions that surged upon the land. 5th, Theological chants of considerable length that can scarcely be called songs at all, containing as they do regular ethical essays. 6th Ceremonial songs, belonging chiefly to the Hill tribes. The Badaga and Coorg songs of this class are especially worthy of attention. Interesting examples will appear in the following pages. 7th, Labor songs, only met with among the working classes. They are generally composed in the vulgar dialect, and scorn the restraints of grammar and the nice rules of poesy. 8th, Mothers' songs, composed for and sung to children. There are many such, but it is not easy for a European to gather them. All of these classes are represented in the following pages.

There is another class of songs, or rather chanted poems, which has not come within the sphere of this book—the episodes from the Bhagavatam, Mahabharata, Ramayana and the Puranas, which form so large a portion of the public amusements. These are distinct Brahman importations and are in no sense indigenous. They are eagerly listened to, and form the chief means by which the Brahmans plant in the national mind the evidences of their own greatness. Many writers, and notably Mr. Griffiths of Benares, have given attention to and translated them. They do not represent pure Dravidian feeling and therefore do not belong to this subject.

It is the common remark of all who study Dravidian literature that the older it is the purer it is. The fact is induced by the growing influence of the Brahmans. At first warmly repelled, because of the pretensions of the priesthood, it gradually forced its way to the front, as the influence of an educated and closely united class ever will, mainly because it embraces all the higher literature. For a while the fight was evenly maintained, but the foreign element progressed till almost the whole written literature of the country became Brahmanic. Indigenous poetry fell into undeserved contempt or, where that was not possible, was edited so unscrupulously, that the original was hidden under a load of corruption. Take for example the songs of Sivavakyer. Purely deistical and strongly opposed to idolatry and cumbrous ceremonial, they were so vigorous as poetry, so fervid in expressing the inmost feelings of every honest heart, and took such a hold upon the people, that they could not be burked. What followed? The Brahmans have corrupted what they could not destroy. The editing of all books gradually fell to them, because they alone had the leisure and knowledge that literary labor required. To the public demand for Sivavakyer they responded by issuing "expurgated and improved" editions. Each editor added new names and references to Siva or Vishnu, left out further verses from the original, and softened still more the many vigorous phrases. This process was continued till it became almost impossible to discover the original. The Mackenzie MSS. contain but one mutilated copy of a decently pure collection. The only copies that I have been able to purchase are as obscure and overloaded with puranic superstition as the legend of any pagoda. The same thing has occurred with all the best Dravidian poetry. The Gnana Venba cannot be obtained at all, though in the 15th century it was one of the most popular of books. The Tiruvalluva Charitra has been remodelled till it appears that every early

Dravidian writer was a Brahman, although the very object of the book was to show that Tiruvalluva and his fellows were pariahs. Still the book is looked upon as something almost heretical, and this because it seems to show that Brahmans could marry even Pariah women in past ages without loss of caste, and that early literature was chiefly cultivated by the indigenous races.

In the Malayalim country, where Brahmanic influence is most powerful, the greater part of the popular songs have perished without leaving a trace of their existence. Even in the temple services translations from Tamil puranic chants are constantly used. At the other extreme of the social scale, where Brahmanism is only now forcing its way, the hill tribes are musical with ballad, lyric and dirge. They have songs for every event in life. They cut the first sheaves of harvest to a song. They come into life, are married, and die to the music of some chant, song or requiem.

As far as my information extends at present, ballads proper do not exist, except among the hill-tribes. By ballads I understand songs containing a story, in which the catastrophe or triumph is the key to the whole piece. Tho tendency of the national mind is ethical. The Brahmanic importations are usually violently amorous, or extravagantly wild. In neither case is there room for the simple pathetic ballad. Modern Dravidian literature (poetic) is almost confined to the three classes of amorous poems, pagoda sthalams or the legends on which the temples claim sanctity or honor, and songs or rather poems in praise of a particular person or deity. The second class is very numerous, and the demand for them is great. Each pagoda has a grand day or days, the anniversary of the event that is supposed to have led to its foundation, and on these occasions the legend is publicly recited or sold for a few pice to the crowd. Now and then plays are published, and there is now living a Tamil author whose works are very popular. But they are so dreadfully long, requiring several days for their representation, that they cannot possibly be brought within the class of songs. The Tahsildar Natakam (Natakam-play, drama) is the most admired of this class.

But it is now time that the songs should speak for themselves. They are arranged in order of language and subject. As my first introduction to this literature was through the Canarese "Dasarapadas," I give them first. *Pada* is our English word *pad,* Latin *ped-is,* and means a foot, corresponding with the English term of the same meaning. It means a song or poem, because it is composed of feet or goes by paces. *Dasa* means a servant or slave, and is the name given to those who devote themselves or are devoted by their parents to the service of God. They are usually attached to some pagoda or temple and perform all menial duties there. In process of time the *Dasas* or Dasara have become a singing caste and have traditions and customs as other castes. Those not attached to a pagoda usually obtain a livelihood by begging. Not that they are despised or counted disreputable. Far from it. To be a mendicant in the Puranic system is to serve God in the most acceptable method possible.

The first three or four songs describe the attacks of death and the uncertainty of life. The next point out that inward purity is required by God rather than outward service. The third class contain outpourings against the sorrows of life, its pain and darkness. Lastly are several collections of proverbs.

THE NEARNESS OF DEATH.

1. "Oh! what is food to me! Death stands so near!
Morn, noon and night his angels close appear.
In one short day they snatched, as past they ran,
My friend, my foe, the young, the grey-haired man.
Their wealth doth stay behind, although so dear.
There is no joy for me, my life is drear."

Chorus.—How near is death! Mercy he cannot bring.
Then, oh my heart, cease from the world, and cling
With all thy power to tender Lakshmi's* king.

2. "Two days ago the marriage feast was mine;
And only yesterday I bought milch kine
Wherewith to start my modest home. My field
Is bright with corn, with gold my coffers yield,
I cannot die." While yet thou speakest, fool,
Dread Yama's† step comes near. Farewell, vile soul.

Chorus.—How near is death! &c.

* Lakshmi the goddess of beauty and wife of Vishnu.

† Yama, the god of the regions of the dead—the agent employed by the higher Gods for carrying mortals away from earth to Hades.

3. "My house is newly built. E'en now they say
The mantras* that have power to drive away
All evils from my home. My wife is great
With child. The day that weds my son we wait.
Life is so good, I cannot, will not, die."
Vain fool! Death's hand now shades thy glazing eye.
Chorus.—How near is death! &c.

4. "To-day the milk boils with the rice. We feast
The birth-day of our son. The next bright east
Will see the sacred thread† by priests thrown o'er
The shoulders of my heir." Oh, trouble sore!
Thou say'st, "Thou canst not die." Behind thy back
Death stands and laughs, and fears not to attack.
Chorus.—How near is death! &c.

5. He will not give you time. You may not eat
The rice that now stands cooked. Your eager feet
May bring no helping friends. Accounts must stay
Unpaid. In short, my friend, you must obey
When death doth call. Oh, heart, my trembling heart,
Think well on Vishnu's god-like feet. From him ne'er part.
Chorus.—How near is death! &c.

* Magic sentences, generally unintelligible to the people. These sentences are said to have the most miraculous power. Even the Hindoo trinity are supposed unable to resist their operation.

† Brahmans, Vaisyas and the higher Sudra castes always carry a number of threads, loosely fastened together, forming a string which hangs over the left shoulder down to the waist. Investiture with the thread is the entrance into manhood and conveys permission to join in all religious ceremonies. It is said to represent a new birth, something like the baptismal regeneration of certain Christian sects. After the ceremony, the young Brahman receives the title of "the twice born."

DEATH.

1. He will not give you time to eat cooked rice,
Nor dun the gull whose note you've filed;
No jewels from the box may make you nice:—
For Yama* gives no time.

Chorus.—Although you love your body, trust it not,
But strive to gain due merit for thy lot.
Thy lusty strength cannot avail one jot.

2. You wish to call your sister to your side,
And bid farewell to wife and child;
To shed salt tears for facts from dreams so wide:—
But Yama gives no time.

Chorus.—Although you love your body, &c.

3. You cry that friends must not be left so soon,
That pulse and ghee to priests you'll send,
The marriage of thy son waits but new moon:—
Yet Yama gives no time.

Chorus.—Although you love your body, &c.

4. Your house is high, it seems the skies to touch—
Your purse is full, you ought to spend—
Your elephants and men want watching much:—
Still Yama gives no time.

Chorus.—Although you love your body, &c.

5. Your strength, you think, will ever stand your part;
Yet worse than useless will it prove.
Let Purandála see a loving heart:—
Then Yama brings no fear.

Chorus.—Although you love your body, &c.

* Yama, the God of death and the infernal regions—the Indian representative of Pluto.

THE BEST FRIEND.

1. One begs of others for a wife,
   On her bestows both rule and home,
   He counts her half of all his life.
   But when death comes, he dies alone.

   Chorus.—Of all good things the best are three—
   Wives, lands, and countless gain.
   Which is the dearest friend to thee?

2. One mounts the throne of mighty kings,
   His palace girds with fort and wall;
   Of his great power the whole world rings.
   His lifeless corse to dogs will fall.

   Chorus.—Of all good things, &c.

3. King's grace, good luck, hard work and trade,
   May load with wealth of coin or land.
   What tyrants leave, the moths invade;
   For riches fly like desert sand.

   Chorus.—Of all good things, &c.

4. In vain wives mourn, in vain sons weep,
   Wealth helps e'en less in death's last scene.
   Two things alone the gulf can leap—
   The sin, the good, our life has seen.

   Chorus.—Of all good things, &c.

5. In this weak frame put not your trust,
   But think on Him with inward calm.
   Is your heart clean? For Him you lust?
   Then Vishnu is a healing balm.

   Chorus.—Of all good things, &c.

LIFE.

1. If men have no health, Sir,
   What good is their wealth?
   If men have no wealth, Sir,
   What good is their health?
   If both of the twain should o'er him reign
   Do you think a good wife he will gain?

Chorus.—Oh, Vishnu, thou wilt never give
Thy grace—the good man's vital breath—
To those who still in sin do live,
Whose feet run in the way to death.

2. Our frame is a house, Sir,
   Short notice we get.
   Our wives have the nous, Sir,
   Examples they set.
   Our houses we quit, like smoke we flit,
   But the next is as bad or worse fit.

Chorus.—Oh, Vishnu, &c.

3. If life you will trust, Sir,
   Old Scratch will you nab.
   To death go you must, Sir,
   Your alms he will grab.*
   "To-morrow" you say—'tis just your way—
   My advice is but this, give to-day.

Chorus—Oh, Vishnu, &c.

* The Poet refers to the world-wide practice of trying to buy off death and future punishment by a charity that only begins when the hand can no longer hold the wealth that it has laid up. He graphically describes how the dying man is still reluctant to pay the very bribe he promises—he will give "to-morrow."

4. Oh, where will you be, Sir,
   In twenty-four hours?
Grim death you will see, Sir,
   Your pleasure it sours.
You say you wont go? I'm sure you know
How they* grin as they hear you say so.
Chorus.—Oh, Vishnu, &c.

5. You see that men die, Sir,
   How sick you soon grow!
You cannot tell why, Sir,
   In turn you must go.
"That's mine, this is thine"—such is his whine.
Better pray, so I say, while there's time.
Chorus.—Oh, Vishnu, &c.

6. Oh man, only dust, Sir,
   A weak broken reed!
If flesh you would trust, Sir,
   A friend you will need.
In Vishnu you'll find a tender mind,
Take his feet to your heart—he'll be kind.
Chorus.—Oh, Vishnu, &c.

We now come to a series of the highest moral character, exhibiting a purity of doctrine which is the last thing most persons would expect to see in Hindoo literature. The thought will often intrude itself that here we find a standard of religious duty almost unknown to the world, as intended for the masses, except in the New Testament. Equally frequent will be

* The angels of death, sent forth to gather in the lost soul.

the reflection that Brahmanism, that is Puranism, never could produce such works, and that the songs exhibit a spiritual tone which makes one deeply regret that there is so little left of indigenous Dravidian literature. The songs that follow are but samples of a considerable mass. It is odd indeed to hear them chanted, as I first did, in the entrance hall of a pagoda dedicated to Hanuman, the monkey deity who so greatly aided Rama in his search for Sita. The Bhagavat Gita contains noble descriptions of the deity, but has no conception of faith. On the contrary it teaches that the highest human duty is that of meditation and the strictest ceremonial observance. The first of the series fitly introduces the rest, in strains that, even in a feeble translation, send a thrill of pleasant recognition through the Christian mind.

TRUE PURITY.

1. Oh, wouldst thou know in what consists
The purity which keeps the soul ?
Behold the things the good resists,
The works that make the wounded whole.

Chorus.—Oh man, why boastest thou in pride,
The smallness of thy mind to screen ?
Go, bathe thy vile polluted hide
In meditation's sacred stream.

2. Thy parents honor and obey,
Release the prisoner from his chain,
In Heaven's road for ever stay,
And think on Vishnu's wondrous reign.

Chorus.—Oh man, &c.

3. The common woman hate and scorn,
   At neighbour's head no hard words send,
With honesty thy life adorn,
   Desire the things which please thy friend.

Chorus.—Oh man, &c.

4. Examine oft thy inner self,
   Deal justly in the market seat,
Proclaim the truth at loss of pelf,
   Think long on Hari's golden feet.

Chorus.—Oh man, &c.

5. With good men let thy life be spent,
   True wisdom strive to understand,
Read oft the Shastras God hath sent,
   And seek for good from Vishnu's hand.

Chorus.—Oh man, &c.

6. Pay soon thy vows at sacred shrine,
   Despise not e'en the lowliest thing,
Of evil eye fear not the shine,
   But meditate on Lakshmi's king.

Chorus.—Oh man, &c

7. Abhor the pride that falsely tells
   That thou art good and clean,
And bathe thy soul in sacred wells
   From meditation's stream.

Chorus.—Oh man, &c.

The next song contains an attempt to render into English one of the most characteristic Dravidian metres. A certain consonant is selected to begin the first line of the verse. In the next line that consonant heads the second syllable. In the third line it commences the third syllable, and so on. To employ this metre literally would be both difficult and useless, as English readers rely upon accent or rhyme alone and the repetition of the letter would catch neither eye nor ear. I have, therefore, substituted accent, and it will be found that with each line of the song the accent moves forward one syllable. The chorus is excepted.

PURITY IN THE SIGHT OF GOD.

1. Purification before the Great God
Is greater than life and is stronger than death—
'Tis the hope of the wise, 'tis the prize of the saint.
Where is the fount from which comes the pure stream?

Chorus.—What profit can the sinner find
In washing oft? How vain the care!
God knows full well—He sees the mind—
That true devotion dwells not there.

2. Alms-giving lies at the base of the steps
That lead to the height from which purity flows.
To know wisdom and truth, and thy lusts to forsake,
Trust in thy God—meditate on His grace.

Chorus.—What profit, &c.

3. Drink the foul water in which have been washed
The feet of thy guru, and honor the words
Of thine elders and priests; to thy guests give thy best;
Cling above all to the feet of thy God.

Chorus.—What profit, &c.

4. Purification must bring in its course
The hate of the bad and the love of the good.
'Twill bring freedom from prick of the conscience for sin
Union with God in his mercy and love.

Chorus.—What profit, &c.

The two songs that follow are pure metaphor, adapted to a high religious purpose. The first deals with the *name* of God, which is described as being sweeter than aught else to the man who loves and fears the deity.

THE NAME OF GOD.

1. My stock is not packed on the backs of strong kine,
Nor pressed into bags strongly fastened with twine.
Wherever it goes it no taxes doth pay,
But still is most sweet, and brings profit, I say.

Chorus.—Oh, buy sugar-candy, my candy so good,
For those who have tasted say nought is so sweet
As the honey-like name of the Godlike Vishnu.

2. It wastes not with time, never gives a bad smell.
You've nothing to pay, though you take it right well.
White ants cannot eat the fine sugar with me.
The city resounds as its virtues men see.

Chorus.—Oh, buy sugar-candy, &c.

3. From market to market it is needless to run,
The shops know it not, the bazaar can have none.
My candy, you see, is the name of Vishnu,
So sweet to the tongue that gives praise as is due.

Chorus.—Oh, buy sugar-candy, &c.

COOKED RICE.

1. Take virtue for your boiling pot,
Pour water cleansed with holiness,
With speed—a mind that wavers not—
Let honor strain the steaming mess.

Chorus.—Be sure you take cooked rice with you,
Take pains to pack cooked rice, pray do.
Your joy will be beyond all price
If you but pack enough cooked rice.

2. Spread wisdom's cloth, so free from taint,
And sprinkle curds of manner grave.
Then with the grace of firm restraint
To Hari offer all He gave.

Chorus.—Be sure you take, &c.

3. Great Vishnu is my stock of food,
My bag of rice so oft untied.
Each day I eat—'tis always good.
All those who eat are satisfied.

Chorus.—Be sure you take, &c.

We now turn to one of the bitterest pieces of satire that can anywhere be met with. The contrast of style and matter with those that have preceded it is very striking ; yet it cannot be called illnatured, for it points at a class and not at individuals. Each verse contains an antithesis, comparing sinful deeds with the hypocritical religious fervour so often employed either to conceal or expiate a sin which is still continued. The first two lines contain the vice, the last two the sanctimonious zeal which is intended to hoodwink both God and man.

WHY I LAUGH.

1. One night I saw a man
   Kissing a harlot's lips.
 Next morn to bathe he ran,
   And prayed on finger tips !*

Chorus.—Oh, how I laugh ! I laugh out loud.
   It makes me laugh to see the crowd,
   Such tricks they do. I oft have vowed
   I'd laugh no more: with it I'm bowed.

2. A woman left her house
   And joined a man as mean.
 She made a thousand vows
   And washed at holy stream !

Chorus.—Oh, how I laugh ! &c.

3. I saw one live in lust,
   His gentle words were few.
 He fed upon a crust,
   And thought upon Vishnu !

Chorus.—Oh, how I laugh ! &c.

CEREMONIAL NOT RELIGION.

1. You bathe, in meditation pass the day,
 And sit or stand as still as any crane !
 You meditate ? A foolish dream, I say !
 Can Krishna, who himself cut short the reign
 Of demons and their imps, love aught but deeds ?

* He counted on his fingers the prayers he uttered that he might be sure he omitted none and thus performed his full religious duty.

Chorus.—'Tis surely worse than fool would do,
To flog and starve thy fleshly part;
When thou hast never set thy heart
On Lakshmi's Lord, the great Vishnu.

2. What good can come from sitting like a bear
And crying ever—"I will pray, will pray;"
Yet, to escape a bore, will count each prayer?
One prayer alone yields fruit, and that for aye—
The great and goodly name, Naráyana.

Chorus.—'Tis surely worse than fool would do, &c.

3. Oh God, didst thou not in the former time
Forgive Jamila's sins, in that his tongue*
Gave forth thy name? Oh Soul, what doubts are thine
And fears! O stay not, flee at once, as stung
By snake or bee. Keep Vishnu in thy view.

Chorus.—'Tis surely worse than fool would do, &c.

GOD THE SAVIOUR.

1. When proud Komava raised the robe
That covered Draupad's charms,†
Her five brave husbands, mad with rage,
Were helpless to protect.
Oh, Hari, thou wast near to save.
How strong art thou and brave!

* This refers to a popular legend regarding a notorious thief. He was one day surprised by a tiger, and in his fright ejaculated the words "Oh Hari, Hari." The God immediately sent help and relieved Jamila from his danger. The robber was so grateful for the divine interposition that he erected a shrine on the spot and became an ascetic.

† This is a well known incident in the story of the Pandus as related in the Mahabbarata. Each verse that follows contains a similar reference. The Dravidian poet draws a useful lesson from the Brahmanic legends.

Chorus.—If Hari be not mine,
Who else can help or see ?
Oh, Hari, grace and strength are thine.
Be ever near to me !

2. If thou, oh father, hadst not come,
Great Vishnu's sword in hand,
And split the gaping monster's mouth
The friendly king had died.
Oh Vishnu, who can save like thee?
So great thy help and free !

Chorus.—If Hari be not mine, &c.

3. When Agmilanu broke his caste
Death's Angels shadowed him.
Yet thou, O Lord of worlds, didst hear
His weeping children's cry.
How swift thy Angels flew to help !
His life was from thyself.

Chorus.—If Hari be not mine, &c.

OUTWARD RITES NOT RELIGION.

1. Oh Soul ! What good can Ganges give ?
Can water cleanse, or thinking long
On God ? When still thy feet choose sin,
And merit springs not from thy deeds.

Chorus.—Oh heart ! My heart ! How vile art thou !
No hound more mad than thou art now.
Can folly bring thee peace or praise ?
Then turn, oh fool, and lift thy gaze
To never dying Vishnu's feet.

2. When guile o'erspreads thy crooked path,
   And inward sin kills holy zeal,
Can prayer make clean thy soul, or whips
   Drive out the foulness from thy heart?
Chorus.—Oh heart! &c.

3. Why hide thy face or pull thy nose,*
   Do all that Brahman law commands?
When He who on the serpent rests
   Can hear no praise, no worship see.
Chorus.—Oh heart! &c.

4. "A priest I am. My life is spent
   In searching long for sacred shrines."
Go to, Oh fool! A priest is he
   Who humbly learns and holy lives.
Chorus.—Oh heart! &c.

5. Not in the smoke of sacrifice,
   Nor in the chant of Vedic hymns,
Does God look for the lowly mind
   That fitly enters into bliss.
Chorus.—Oh heart! &c.

6. The fiery God is found by those
   Who lust no more—who feel no pride—
Whose senses close 'gainst sin and self—
   Who humbly walk before their God.
Chorus.—Oh heart! &c.

* Both phrases describe a portion of the daily ceremonial of the Brahmans. In the morning ablutions it is necessary to close every aperture of the body; thus, among other things, the Brahman covers his face, so that he may be sure he has closed eyes, nose, mouth and ears. A subsequent ritual requires that the devotee should pass his thumb and forefinger down both sides of the nose. The author insinuates that, to be quite sure that he has duly saluted his nose, the Pharisaic devotee firmly grasps the organ, pulling it smartly and frequently.

7. What good can come from earthly toil?
   Whence can the root of merit spring?
If, oh my soul, thy grasp be weak,
   Or wandering thoughts let Vishnu slip.

Chorus.—Oh heart! &c.

BODY AND SOUL.

1. Skin covers flesh and blood and bone:
Within are worms, excretions vile,
Disease and spirits evil, pain and moan.
Thy strength, oh man, is death and hell.

Chorus.—Think not this flesh will bide,
On earth shall find its goal.
But love the lotus-eyed;
In him find peace, O soul.

2. You love your child, your friend, your wife,—
'Tis joy you say; 'tis sin you know.
Forego this joy, it steals your life,
And think on Him who saves from woe.

Chorus.—Think not this flesh will bide, &c.

3. Serve Brahma* first, your neighbour love,
Avoid a harlot as a sword;
Go where they praise the Lord above,
And shout—"Oh, Hari, Hari, Lord!"

Chorus.—Think not this flesh will bide, &c.

* In this and similar phrases, the word Brahma must not be supposed to refer to the first person of the Hindu Triad. It is always used in the neuter as a sort of scientific term for the Deity, and has no connection with the personal masculine Brahma.

4. Purandala Vithâla, help!
If thou hast e'er extended grace,
Give it to me, give me thyself.
For this is joy—to see thy face.

Chorus.—Think not this flesh will bide, &c.

The song "How to cross the sea of sin" introduces a group perhaps the most characteristic of Dravidian literature and character. It has been common among western thinkers to look upon the theory of the transmigration of souls as eminently comforting to those who trust in it. Here we see the direct contrary taught by the most convincing testimony. It gives no rest either in the present or the future. But the human soul craves for rest, even in suffering, as the highest good. I venture to say "even in suffering," because every heart that fears the future instinctively cries "let me know the worst." Transmigration can never reveal the worst. The punishment of sin in this life is a more degraded life still. That inevitably leads to something yet more to be dreaded. Thus the future is a long cumulation of woe, almost without one redeeming ray of light; for where mercy can only be earned by merit the wicked have no hope. Note the bitter cry:—

"How many births are past I cannot tell.
How many yet may be, no man may say.
But this alone I know, and know full well,
That pain and grief embitter all the way."

Still more grievous is the opening of another appeal against the fate that has made man what he is :—

"A weary and broken down man,
With sorrow I come to thy feet ;
Subdued by the fate and the ban
That hides the long future I meet.
I suffer, without ceasing, the pain
Of sorrowful infinite life."

And again

"Earth's pains I cannot bear,
More still await me there."

In these and similar expressions we seem to meet the utmost of human woe—despair. If transmigration could give ultimate hope it might be well ; but it robs such hope as might otherwise be. A bad man may become a dog or a horse or perhaps a lizard. Let the soul do well there, and it may enter the human frame again. This sounds like hope, but it gives none. It is a million times easier to be a good dog than a good man, and down again goes the poor lost soul, lower than ever before.

Life is a "sea of sin." With sin come trouble and pain. Life is agony and sorrow. There is no rest, now and hereafter. Such is the sad Dravidian creed. The Tamil "Songs of sorrow" have already been referred to. The Telugu Vemana in some thousands of verses does not contain one broad laugh. Some minds cannot bear such darkness. If virtue can bring no rest, if abstinence in this world cannot ensure pleasure in the next, and anyhow the soul must go down into the dark abyss of the future, why not fly to the pleasure that is within our reach? While we live, let us live.

Out of this reaction has grown a glorification of pleasure, of sexual enjoyment, of every kind of sensual gratification. Even the great and good Tiruvalluva has written in "Praise of lust." Let us pity rather than blame. Puranism grasped the worse school, deified vice and created a Krishna. It conquered because it was aided by three potent allies—the superior intelligence and knowledge of the Brahmans, the ignorance and necessary hesitation of their victims, and its glorification of human licence. The Tamils are the most civilized Dravidian people,—among them chiefly do we find outspoken rampant sensuality under the guise of religion. It is, however, necessary to bear in mind that sensual enjoyment is not necessarily immoral. Tiruvalluva's "Praise of Lust" would be grievously misunderstood if it were supposed to exalt indiscriminate harlotry. He constantly requires that men should live with their own wives and "hate a harlot as a sword." Where pleasure of any kind may legitimately be enjoyed, Tiruvalluva and many other writers believe that it may be eulogized, may be described in detail. They act on the principle that it cannot logically be wrong to describe what every one may experience. The hill tribes are the least Brahmanized, among them sensuality is never glorified. Between these extremes are the Canarese,—their songs will show their views.

HOW TO CROSS THE SEA OF SIN.

A FATHER'S ADVICE.

1. Our life is but a sea of sorrow,
This comes, that goes, the old old way.
No joy will last beyond to-morrow,
E'en grief and pain—they will not stay.
Why should we run such things to meet,
Or set our hearts on things so fleet?
One thing alone is worth a nod—
To touch the heart of Lakshmi's God.

Chorus.—Oh, sons of mine, how shall we win
Across the fearful sea of sin?
Oh sons, shout loud Naráyana.
Lakshmi's king, my sons, Naráyana.

2. The strength obtained by food will fail,
So will the gold which fills your purse.
The glories of your house will pale,
Your lofty fort may prove a curse.
Not one of these will serve you well
To fight against the king of hell.
Then, sons of mine, your voices raise
In world-renowned Vishnu's praise.

Chorus.—Oh, sons of mine, &c.

3. Some play at dice, and some at chess,
Some plague the wife and she plagues some.
Some with great wealth their souls would bless.
To one sure end they all will come.
The infernal God will catch them all,
Who Vishnu's name forget to call.
In Narasimha's lovely face
Lay all your hopes of future grace.

Chorus.—Oh, sons of mine, &c.

4. Don't be too fond of wife or girls
Or laugh because thy sons are three.
For when grim death his life-wheel twirls*
The stern demand will come for thee.
Of Maya† never be the slave
Else thou wilt not the death-god brave.
Adore the God that sleeps on sea,
And endless bliss thy lot shall be.

Chorus.—Oh, sons of mine, &c.

5. In pride or strength, in hate or love,
In wealth or goods put not your trust.
Embrace the feet of God above,
Or else your hopes will turn to dust.
Long thought on God will steel the mind
Against the ills which all men find.
And if thy sorrows thou wouldst heal
To glorious Vishnu ever kneel.

Chorus.—Oh, sons of mine, &c.

* This is an old Aryan figure. Death is a lottery. How else can be explained the seeming cruelty which takes the young and leaves the old; that carries away the bread-winner and permits the bread-eater to continue his useless life? Our names are shaken together in a whirling box, and that which comes out first belongs to the next victim of the grisly king.

† The proper meaning of the word is "that which is not self-existent." As all things depend on God, can be made or unmade at His pleasure, it is a mistake to look upon matter as having any goodness or power. God is all in all. Every thing is but a shadow of Him. But ignorant men cannot see this. They live for the world. To them the world is everything and God is nothing. They are victims of Maya.

A CRY FOR HELP.

1. How many births are past I cannot tell,
How many yet may be, no man may say.
But this alone I know, and know full well,
That pain and grief embitter all the way.
My woes are more than I can bear, but thou,
Great God, who once didst bless e'en Ibharaj,*
Of elephants the king, canst help me now.
Be pleased to grant my prayer—my soul enlarge.

Chorus.—Oh Vishnu, help! Great Vishnu, Save
A wretched soul like mine!
Thou holdest up the earth and wave,
Oh, send thy aid in time.

2. Great Lord, my boyish years were one long pain,
Although they seemed to pass in play. For play
Is nought but pain, in that it brings disdain
Of God and holy things. This very day,
Thou happy Narasimha,† hear my prayer
And freely, from thy heart, on me bestow
The help that now to ask I humbly dare.
Oh, help and save before from life I go!

Chorus.—Oh Vishnu, help! Great Vishnu, Save, &c.

3. But now, in age and feebleness extreme,
Distress and pain are harder still to bear.
I cannot bear such woe. 'Tis like a stream
That surges over-head. Dost thou not care,

* The story of Ibhâraj the king of elephants is similar to that of Jamila.

† Narasimha, the man-lion, the fourth incarnation of Vishnu.

Purandala Vithala, in whose eye
All men are one and equal ? On thy throne,
Oh king of birds, how swiftly dost thou fly !*
List, hear with joy, and take me for thy own.

Chorus.—Oh Vishnu, help! Great Vishnu, Save, &c.

LIFE'S SORROW.

1. A weary and broken down man,
With sorrow I come to thy feet,
Subdued by the fate and the ban
That hides the long future I meet.
I suffer, without ceasing, the pain
Of sorrowful infinite life.
Thou never canst listen in vain
To earnest and soul-yearning strife.

Chorus.—Govinda,† thy feet are my part.
Come, tread on the ground of my heart.
I'll always remain where thou art.

2. I counted as dearest on earth
Fair women, great wealth and wide land:
And saw not the joy and the worth
Of merited grace from thy hand.

* All the Puranic deities are seated on some animal, showing figuratively that all nature serves them. Vishnu's throne is an eagle. Ganesa is always seated on a rat.

† A name of Krishna, the eighth incarnation of Vishnu. It means—"He that looks after the cows"—and refers to Krishna's infancy, when he was brought up by a tribe of cowherds.

Fell Maya* came in with my birth—
What physic can cure or can save?
With waters of wisdom begirth,
Oh, drown my poor soul in the wave.

Chorus.—Govinda, thy feet are my part, &c.

3 All sins I have done in the past
Now, now make them clean and forgot.
And long as the future may last
Let heavenly life be my lot.
On Vishnu's bright feet ever cast
A longing and confident glance:
And thus wilt thou gain and hold fast
A taste of the bliss in advance.

Chorus.—Govinda, thy feet are my part, &c.

THIS TROUBLESOME WORLD.

1. If thou shouldst have a wife,
Trouble is thine.
If none should bless thy life,
Trouble is thine.
If neither wise nor witty,
Sorrow will come.
Still more if she be pretty,
Sorrow will come.

* The doctrine usually though incorrectly rendered "illusion." It teaches that this earth leads its inhabitants astray, causing them to forget God, seeing that it seems so much nearer and is so much dearer to the sinful soul. See note on page 37.

For then, all guarding vain,
Sore trouble this.
She brings unmeasured pain,
Sore trouble this.

Chorus—Never, oh my soul, can peace be thine
Until great Runga's* grace be mine.
If angry He, all hope resign.

2. If children come to thee,
Sorrow comes too.
But if no heir should be,†
Sorrow comes too.
With earning wealth and power,
Pain fills the cup.
But when the wretched poor—
Pain fills the cup.
Complains he has no rice—
'Tis dolor sore.
Wherewith to sacrifice—
'Tis dolor sore.
No sorrow, pain, or care,
E'en sorrow deep.
Can be so hard to bear,
E'en sorrow deep.

Chorus—Never, oh my soul, &c.

* Yet another name for Vishnu and meaning probably "he that flies swiftly;" referring to the wonderful speed of light as it issues from the sun. Vishnu under the name of Hari is both the sun and the light.

† English readers can have little idea of the yearning of every Hindoo couple for a son. It is universally believed that the future of the dead is without hope if certain ceremonies are not performed at the cremation and on each succeeding anniversary of that occasion. These ceremonies can only be perfectly performed by a son. If there be no son, the whole series of ancestors is debarred from absorption and rest throughout all ages. Hence the necessity of adopting a son if none be born to the house.

3. When men are sick and poor,
Sorrow enters.
Though wealth should bar the door,
Sorrow enters.
If, gained by strength and care,
Pain is in store.
Great hoards the shelves should bear,
Pain is in store.
But if each day you pray,
No sorrow comes.
To him who hears alway,
No sorrow comes.
The excellent Vishnu,
Your joy is great.
Great peace will dwell in you,
Your joy is great.

Chorus—Never, oh my soul, &c.

THE PAINFUL SERVANT.

1. Some pains may not be seen,
They show no wound, I ween,
Although so deep and keen
Oh, fearful pain!
No woman some hath wrought,
Some come from want of thought,
A few go soon as brought.
Such pains are mine.

Chorus.—Oh, dreadful pain! I can't bear pain.
In mercy, Vishnu, save me!

2. My stomach gives me pain,
Bad friends bring it like rain,
Deep trouble leaves the stain.
Oh, cruel pain!
Great pain may come from friend,
Abuse no balm can mend,
Bad men deep pain will send.
Such pains are mine.

Chorus.—Oh, dreadful pain, &c.

3. What pain comes to the poor,
Breached promise addeth more,
To rule oneself is sore.
Oh, biting pain!
Earth's pains I cannot bear,
More still await me there.
Distress must follow care.
Such pains are mine.

Chorus.—Oh, dreadful pain, &c.

4. To be, and not to be,
To see, and not to see,
Are troubles sore to me.
Oh, burning pain!
Oh, Vishnu, let me know
Why pain doth plague me so,
And joy so soon doth go.
Hear my prayer.

Chorus.—Oh, dreadful pain, &c.

FATE.

1. Each house within the village bounds
   Contains some early friend,
   But though in each the food-gong sounds
   No rice to me they lend.
   When sad I walk the village street
   To me they come not near,
   And when I strive my priest to meet
   He starts from me in fear.
   Oh *Hari, Hari, Lakshmi's King,
   Their stare is maddening.

   Chorus.—Oh, whither can I flee for aid ?
   For sin I now am cursed.
   The dread decree by Brahma made†
   May never be reversed.

2. When hunger gnaws my life away
   To dearest friend I go,
   For food and drink I humbly pray—
   Oh God, why hate me so ?—
   They flee from me, their food they hide,
   An empty house I find.

* Hari is one of the most popular names of Vishnu and his incarnation Krishna. It originally meant "green," and then was used to describe anything beautiful and bright. Thus it came to mean the sun. Vishnu has superseded Surya as the sun-god, and in some of the songs that follow is called "the disc of the sun."

† In consequence of sin in a former birth the unfortunate man is doomed by Brahma to be an outcaste. It was unalterable fate that drove him to commit the deed for which he has been cursed and rejected by both God and man. This curse must be worked out.

The sugar-cane which then I spied—
What joy was in my mind!—
Oh Hari, Hari, Lakshmi's King,
How poisonous the thing!

Chorus.—Oh, whither, &c.

3. In dreadful heat, for shade I pine,
And sit beneath a tree.
Still worse on me the sun doth shine.
The curse is there on me.
With burning thirst about to die
I flee to well and lake.
Before my eyes they fail and dry,
No comfort may I take.
Oh Hari, Hari, Lakshmi's King,
Sweet death to me soon bring.

Chorus.—Oh, whither, &c.

4. Before my house rich plantains grow,
I may not eat of one.
My fate is written on my brow*
And cannot be undone.
To thee I turn, for refuge seek,
And cry—"Have mercy, Lord!"
To stem the water flood too weak—
Oh save me by thy word.
Oh Hari, Hari, Lakshmi's King,
Let me of pardon sing.

Chorus.—Oh, whither, &c.

* The curse noted above is written by the finger of God on the forehead of the unhappy sinner. Man cannot read it. Compare the mark of the beast in the Apocalypse.

5. No money can I give to thee,
No breath have I to pray.
So sore distress has come to me
To live I see no way.
Oh God, most perfect God, look down
On one so poor as I.
No other hope I have. I drown
While thou, Oh God, art nigh.
Oh Hari, Hari, Lakshmi's King,
Close to thy feet I cling.

Chorus.—Oh, whither, &c.

THE COURSE OF LIFE.

1. Within my father's frame three months I passed,*
And then, unknowing, came to mother's womb.
For nine long months—each day was as the last—
I burned with pain within my living tomb.
Before I knew my fate a year had gone—
A year of pain. Oh Indra, Hear my moan!

Chorus.—Oh, Sir, my youth is past, my youth is past!

2. Immured in darkness, vows I made to thee;
But sorrow in my birth made me forget.
When childhood came, not yet from sorrow free,
To ease my pain my earnest mind was set.
The filth of self made hell to gape around;
Yet still I knew thee not—to earth was bound.

Chorus.—Oh, Sir, my youth is past, &c.

* It is a popular idea that life commences twelve months before birth, and that the time is spent in the manner described in the text.

3. My boyhood came. The dreams of sixteen years
Ran through my soul. The sports of boys
Drew me from thee. My follies drowned my fears,
And lust enticed me on. I drew my joys
From earth. Oh Vishnu ! God ! whose feet I left,
My sorrow hear, who am of hope bereft.

Chorus.— Oh, Sir, my youth is past, &c.

4. I grew to manhood, tall and straight as palm,
Made friends with elders, middle-aged and youth.
I went from house to house. Without a qualm
My life I spent, nor feared nor sought the truth.
I fell—the sea of sin was ever nigh—
And lost the sweetness of thy lotus-eye.

Chorus.—Oh, Sir, my youth is past, &c.

5. Now, old and imbecile, I groan with pain,*
And sink beneath the swelling of the wave.
Paràndalà† Vithàla, Lord, disdain
Me not, but take me in the ship I crave—
The sturdy ship, by meditation built.
Save quickly, Lord of Lakshmi ! Cleanse my guilt !

Chorus.—Oh, Sir, my youth is past, &c.

* The whole of this song deserves notice. How distinct is its coloring ! How sad must they be whose feelings it represents ! Every stage of life is full of evil—of evil that cannot be avoided, although its penalty is exacted to the uttermost farthing. It should be noted that the one deity is invoked under three names. Indra is the old Vedic deity, but is only known now to the Vaishnava as another name for Vishnu, who has usurped the dignity of his majestic predecessor.

† A local name for Vishnu.

NO HELP BUT IN GOD.

1. I worshipped a stone I could see and could feel,
And therefore have now neither strength nor ally.
I visited oft with the fool and the rogue,
And, like a mad elephant, wounded my friends.
Was wise but for folly; in sinning was brave.
Oh Vishnu, Lord, speedily save!

Chorus.—I see how foolish I have been
And cry against the dread Vishnu—
"Oh, wilt thou never mark the scene
Of strife and sorrow so undue."

2. I made many vows and am weary of sin,
For nothing delights or can profit me now
Each temple I've circled and circled again
Till, weary and worn, I am worse than before,
And nothing is left but thy love or the grave.
Oh Hari, Lord, speedily save!

Chorus.—I see how foolish I have been, &c.

3. The quack and the fool were as gurus to me,
So simple was I, so defiled and un[illegible]hen.
Purándala's grace I now strive to obtain,
So pure and so good, ever worthy of praise.
Thou canst not refuse the protection I crave.
Oh Hari, Lord, speedily save!

Chorus.—I see how foolish I have been, &c.

There follow a series of songs which vividly remind of the Proverbs of Solomon. Both are intended for singing, and both have arranged themselves rather by the demands of metre and consonance than by any connected argument. The Dravidian languages are wonderfully rich in proverbs. In the Tamil language alone the Rev. P. Percival has collected about four thousand five hundred proverbs in common use. In Tanjore the Rev. G. Fryar has gathered nearly as many in the same language. Of course many are to be found in both collections, but after careful comparison it appears that the two earnest missionaries named above have noted and translated not less than six thousand independent proverbs. Each couplet, and sometimes each line, of the following is a proverb.

FOLLY

1. From the open sinner
   Hide what good you can.
   Say not words of wisdom
   To an angry man.

Chorus.—Do not spout your verses
In the public way:
Lest the world compare them
With a poet's lay.
From the heap beside him
Folly took a clod,
Bowed his head before it,
Thought he saw a God.

2. Who mends a broken pot—
   Lifts it from the ground ?
He who visits relative
   When his woes abound.
      Chorus.—Do not spout, &c.

3. Vaishnava is hellish
   Praising Siva's name :*
So is he who, falsely,
   Tells of neighbour's shame.
      Chorus.—Do not spout, &c.

4. Who will take to fighting
   When his wife commands ?
He who gives the leisure
   Prattler's tale demands.
      Chorus.—Do not spout, &c.

5. Men who have two faces
   Scorn with hatred strong.
Keshana† the God-like,
   Be thy constant song.
      Chorus.—Do not spout, &c.

* This curious evidence of the strongly monotheistic tendency of the popular mind has been already quoted. A man may worship Vishnu or Siva and no objection will be made. Let him serve both and he is looked upon either as a knave or a fool. The reason of so strange a paradox lies in the presumed necessity that the devotee should have but one God in mind, and He must be esteemed as the supreme being, the incorporeal essence of all things. If the worshipper call that being Vishnu, well. If he call Him Siva, well. But if he use both names he will run great danger of dividing the Deity in his thoughts, and of worshipping two individuals rather than one essence.

† In his fourth incarnation Vishnu took the form of a lion, under the name of Narasimha or the man lion. Hence he is popularly styled Keshana or the lion-maned, from the Sanscrit Kesa, hair.

THE FOOL.

1. The man who leaves his wife and home,
Or trusts relations' love;
Who gives his wealth to friends to mind,
Or stoops to paltry spite.
That man is fool indeed, Sir.

Chorus.—The world is full of foolish folk
Who know not wisdom's worth,—
Forsake their God,—His wrath provoke,—
Bow down to Gods of earth.

2. Who sells his daughter's pride for food,
Or lives with wife's papa;
Who being poor will scold the rich,
Or knows not his own mind.
Such folk are dreadful fools, Sir.

Chorus.—The world is full, &c.

3. Some marry when their hair is gray,
Or joke before a snake;
And some forget their parents' need
And Vishnu's fatherhood.
These, too, are fools, you know, Sir.

Chorus.—The world is full, &c.

4. To Brahmans give, at Kasi bathe,
Are duties strict. So these—
A Dasi be, on Vishnu think.
If one should fail in them,
A fool outright is he, Sir.

Chorus.—The world is full, &c.

5. Who drinks the milk when calf is dead,*
Or lends without a pledge;
Of one concern thinks twenty ways,
Or scorns his mother's love;
Is fool enough for me, Sir.
Chorus.—The world is full, &c.

6. Who worships not the great god Ram,†
Nor good gets from his wealth,
Nor bows beneath his guru's feet,
But takes a sinful bribe;
Must be a wretched fool, Sir.
Chorus.—The world is full, &c.

7. Who lies to him that gives him food,
Or slander spreads around,
Avoids the shrine and hates the name
Of lotus-eyed Vishnu,
Is fool of fools on earth, Sir.
Chorus.—The world is full &c.

The fourth verse of the preceding song is evidently an interpolation, and is an example of the mode in which all indigenous literature has been tampered with.

* The Indian cowherd does not remove the calf from its mother until the supply of milk ceases. Whenever the cow is milked the calf is allowed to suck for a minute or so first. This ensures a proper flow of milk. As soon as sufficient time has been given, the calf is pulled off and tied to the fore leg of the cow. When the man can draw no more he unfastens the calf and allows it to suck what it can. This first taste and last gleaning is all the calf usually receives from its mother after the first month. In consequence of this continued close connection of calf and cow, it is believed to be both wicked and injurious to drink milk obtained from a cow whose calf is dead.

† Ram, or more commonly Rama, is the seventh incarnation of Vishnu, and represents a great warrior, come on earth to overthrow the Kshatriyas.

THE GOOD AND EVIL OF WEALTH.

1. What fills the house with children good,
And gives the taste of sweets and ghee?
What saves from duns and bailiffs rude,
And without which life cannot be?
Sister, it is wealth.

Chorus.—See, sister mine, the sorrows deep,
That hide in wealth's great heap.
Two sorrows dire great wealth must reap.

2. What makes relations' need forgot,
But saves in danger from the foe?
What teaches men to tie a knot,*
And hate all change, as fraught with woe?
Sister, it is wealth.

Chorus.—See, sister mine, the sorrows deep, &c.

3. What makes the foolish wise again,
And passes hosts of bad rupees?†
What sweeter than the sugar-cane,
And if it fly leaves little ease?
Sister, it is wealth.

Chorus.—See, sister mine, the sorrows deep, &c.

* Thus in the original. The knot of course is a moral one, and refers to the complications and artifice which a rich man can throw round his doings to the injury of the poor and weak.

† This illustration is full of meaning in India, where it has always been a favorite occupation of the powerful to debase and clip the coin, trusting to their power and armed servants for impunity.

4. What hides a bad repute, and brings
A crowd of servants, courtiers gay?
What loads with pearls and golden rings
And stays sore trouble in its way?
Sister, it is wealth.

Chorus.—See, sister mine, the sorrows deep, &c.

5. What brings the learned at one's nod,
Yet drives real friends from board and hall?
What causes men to turn from God—
The great Purandala Vithal?
Sister, it is wealth.

Chorus.—See, sister mine, the sorrows deep, &c.

WHAT MATTERS IT?

1. What if the food a man doth hate
Hang high as palm-tree leaves?
Or that the house be wide and great
When the owner no alms gives?
What can it be to you who wait
If office fall to fools?
Or if the bitch beside your gate
Have milk for all she rules?

Chorus.—If earth be full of precious things
But none may come your way,
What matters it?
If when the goat his capers flings
His throat teats dance so gay,
What matters it?

2. What use is handsome face and eyes
To surly son and heir?
Or all the beauty of the skies
To spiteful sharp "grey mare?"
What good or gain in brother lies
If wrathful man he be?
What benefit can e'er arise
If pariah feast one see?

Chorus.—If earth be full of precious things, &c.

3. Why ask the way to here or there,
If that be not thy road?
Or heap up gold and jewels rare,—
A useless worthless load
To him who offers not a prayer
And dares a Saint despise?
For neither rich nor pure can bear
God's wrath 'gainst them to rise.

Chorus.—If earth be full of precious things, &c.

The song on the next page is one of the best specimens of a proverbial series that I have ever met with. Each couplet is a perfect proverb, and many of them are very popular, occurring constantly in the ordinary business of life. The verses are arranged much more systematically than usual. Thus the second and third verses deal particularly with the punishment that certain sins will surely bring home to those who commit them. The fourth and fifth describe the reward that will, equally certainly, be the fortune of those who leave the world and cling to religious duty. The reward may either be bliss in the world to come or freedom from temptation in this. The first verse is a warning that we must not expect impossibilities. The previous songs also deserve attention, giving, as they do, an excellent idea of the every-day morality of the masses of the people. "Poor Richard" has evidently a wider popularity than most scholars have been willing to admit.

WISDOM.

1. If every day with glowing speech you teach the truth,
   Will that give joy to woman's heart?
  If in its lustrous beauty wisdom should be taught,
   Will understanding reach the ass?
  If, bowing low, I kiss a golden idol's feet,
   Will kindly words flow from its mouth?
  If sacred musk be used to make the forehead's mark,
   Will aught but pleasure greet the sense?

Chorus.—Will those who worship not the glory of the sun
   Obtain the peace that springs from mukti won?

2. If truth be lost and falsehood take its hallowed place,
   Can man escape the doom of hell?
  If vicious son should break a loving father's heart,
   Can pardon for such sin be found?
  If sinful man despises that which God hath made,
   Can he o'ercome the world's contempt?
  If one should take his neighbour's goods by guile,
   Will not the burglar steal his own?

Chorus.—Will those, &c.

3. When sinners take delight in scorning godly men,
   Their folly can but hurt themselves.
 Who robs the poor and him whose only friend is God,
   Shall live, yet call for death for pain.
 When sages, for their gain, call folly good and wise,
   The street shall hear them jeered as fools.
 While nightfall guides the thief to rob the rich man's chest
   Who guards the spoil of last night's theft?

Chorus.—Will those, &c.

4. To him whose soul has left this earth to sink in God,
   Can youth or beauty bring a charm?
 Can golden rings or muslins light as air adorn
   The forest yogee* in his filth?
 Does Vishnu leave without content or bliss or peace
   The man who loses all for him?
 Or can the man who worships not the golden feet
   Obtain the peace and bliss he needs?

Chorus.—Will those, &c.

5. Can he whom bonds of sense and earth no more restrain
   Neglect the customs of his sires?
 Or he who knows the Shasters six—Can he, O Brahm—
   Absorption's bliss e'er fail to reach?
 Great Vishnu's favor is a gem of worth: the man
   Who owns need fear no evil eye.
 If thou wouldst reach this bliss, go, kiss the lovely feet
   Of Vishnu, Vilapura's king.

Chorus.—Will those, &c.

* An ascetic who has left the world to retire into some lonely place for meditation and penance. He scorns all the ordinary decencies of life, and usually sits in one posture contemplating his navel or the tip of his nose, so that he may see and know nothing of what passes around him.

The song we read next will come as a surprise to most people. It is, however, much to be feared that in this respect the popular habit follows the advice of the old preacher, and cries—"do as I say, not as I do." If caste estimation depended on personal goodness, India would not have needed the English.

THE TRUE PARIAH.

1. Who guides not his life by the Shastras six,*
   An outcaste will live and will die.
   Who hears not the story of Vishnu's tricks,†
   An outcaste will live and will die.
   The traitor whose cause with his king's dares mix,
   An outcaste will live and will die.
   Who visits the house where the harlot sticks,
   Is outcaste complete in God's eye.

   Chorus.—Beyond the walls the outcastes dwell,
   'Tis worse than death to touch such men.
   What pundit skilled dare ever tell
   How many live within his ken?

2. The man who his debts will not strive to pay,
   A pariah surely must be.
   And he who would walk in a wicked way,
   A pariah surely must be.

* The Shastras are the sacred books and are said to be six in number, but no two sects would agree as to the books they include.

† This word is not used in an offensive sense. The Bhagavatam, one of the most popular of books, is wholly occupied with the "tricks" of Krishna.

So he who a lie to his host will say,
  A pariah surely must be.
In him who his wife for advice will pray,
  Most foolish of pariahs see.

Chorus.—Beyond the walls, &c.

3. The man who is rich but his wealth gives not,
  Is worse than an outcaste indeed.
So he who would poison one's food, I wot,
  Is worse than an outcaste indeed.
Who shuns not the hypocrite's fearful lot,
  Is worse than an outcaste indeed.
But he who would puff his good deeds one jot—
  No outcaste commits such a deed.

Chorus.—Beyond the walls, &c.

4. The man who his promise forgets to keep,
  In pariah village should dwell.
Who sows not the good he desires to reap,
  In pariah village should dwell.
The man who deceives, yet at night can sleep,
  In pariah village should dwell.
Than he who in blood his right-hand dare steep,
  No pariah blacker in hell.

Chorus.—Beyond the walls, &c.

5. Who keeps not the precept that well he knows,
  Is outcaste indeed before God.
On Lakshmi's great lord who does not repose,
  Is outcaste indeed before God.
Who seeing his guru no praise bestows,
  Is outcaste indeed before God.
But he who meets harlot "under the rose"—
  No outcaste so merits the rod.

Chorus.—Beyond the walls, &c.

IGNORANCE.

1. 'Tis ignorance brings the black death to my house,
Her terrible visage embitters my life.
Untrained in a wiser and honester course
The cruel dacoit brings his band to my home.*
Because I'm not wise, with a scandalous tongue,
I steal the fair fame of my neighbour and friend.
An ignorant heart makes me love the false face
Of girls without beauty who dance without grace.†

Chorus.—The ignorant man is a madman indeed.
Hither and thither he rushes, then cuts off his head.

2. This foolishness leads me to plunder my wife
To give all her jewels to prostitute hands;
To think it a pleasure to meet in the street
The woman whose glances are levelled at men.
It leads me to say of the friend of my sire
That virgins by him are oft robbed of their pride.
When means are but small to meet harlot's desire,
It prompts me to steal what may add to her hire.

Chorus.—The ignorant man, &c.

* Dacoity is an important item in the police returns of every part of India. It is gang-burglary. A party of from eight to fifty men proceeds in the night to the house of some rich man and rifles it. Fearless of the police their operations are ostentatiously open, and the only precaution taken is that of so arranging the gang that none shall be known to the inhabitants of the village they rob. Dacoity was the curse of India till the new police system was introduced.

† It must be understood that dancing is an accomplishment peculiar to the Hindu *Hetairæ*. No chaste woman could possibly permit herself to dance.

3. At sight of a greedy and painted old wretch
It makes my heart leap as if loaded with gifts.
I cry like a cat if she come not in time,
And love the vile bonds which prevent my escape.
While under its power do I earnestly strive
For aught that is good, that can bless, or is wise ?
Nay, rather, I love to turn night into day
By swilling with rogues who will praise while I pay.

Chorus.—The ignorant man, &c.

4. When told that my house is infested with rats,
To smoke their retreat I must burn down the house.
If crowds should collect when the evenings are cool,
Of course I am there, and am seized as a thief.
My folly is such that I throw in the ditch
The ashes that ought to be rubbed on my breast.*
Contempt to my caste and the temple I give ;
A Brahman my father, an outcaste I live.

Chorus.—The ignorant man, &c.

5. It persuades me at last my own sons to forget,
And take to my breast dirty brats from a stew.
I swear in the court that a buffalo gives
Quite ten seers of milk, though I know she is dead.
My sword from the scabbard I hasten to draw
To plunge in my bosom—not that of my foe.
Indeed it so lays my best wits on the shelf,—
No enemy else is so bad as myself.

Chorus.—The ignorant man, &c.

* It is a mark of orthodoxy to mark the forehead, breast and arms, with the symbols of Vishnu. The material used is the ashes of sandalwood.

6. My nets when I fish are soon crowded with seer,*
But, having no basket, they rot on the shore.
I rush 'gainst the cobra forgetting my stick,
Am bit for my pains, and most surely will die.
When meeting my creditor's wife in the street,
Her husband and children I load with my curse.
When Yama himself for a victim looks out,
His grip is on me. I must needs give a shout.

Chorus.—The ignorant man, &c.

7. Oh heart, oh my soul, let thy plans come from Him,
Who Lakshmi doth love, and who sleeps on the sea.†
Let pride be forgotten, and praise be thy work;
Then Vishnu will give the true wisdom to you,—
Receive in your service the thanks that are due,—
Will load you with blessings and keep you from death.
Go, sluggard, to view the small ants in the field,
Be humble as they, better thanks should'st thou yield.

Chorus.—The ignorant man, &c.

* The seer is a favorite Indian fish, and in the Madras Presidency is about the size of a good American cod-fish.

† One of the most favorite names of Vishnu is Narayana, meaning "he that rests on the sea." He is represented as reclining on a leaf floating on the water.

BADAGA SONGS.

In the cluster of hills, where the eastern and western Ghauts meet, are embosomed many charming valleys. They afford to the Europeans in India a climate perhaps the most perfect in the world, equally removed from extremes of heat and cold. Coorg and the Wynaad have attracted the planter ; and the virgin forest enframes, so to speak, hundreds of plantations or "estates," chiefly devoted to the growth of coffee, but now containing many an acre of tea and cinchona. The Ooty valley is the best of Indian sanitaria, lacking only, for perfect beauty, such snowy hills as surround and overtop the viceregal Simla. These hills and green plateaus are the home of several mountain tribes. The Kurgis are the highest, the Kotas the lowest in the tribal scale. Below the noblest are the Todas. Above the basest are the Badagas. Other tribes are called Kurumbers and Irulas. They all speak varieties of Hali Cannadi or ancient Canarese, and doubtless represent, almost unchanged, the condition, speech and occupation of the great original stock which has progressed and become civilized in Mysore until it has become what we now see in the Canarese nation. The vocabulary of the dialects is almost pure Aryan, and presents the most startling affinities with the grand Teutonic stock. The grammar is only now beginning to be studied, but will doubtless claim the same relationship.

It seems proper, therefore, that the songs of these older races should follow the Canarese songs previously given, neglecting for the moment the more polished tongues of the plains. We commence, therefore, with a few of the very beautiful chants of the Badaga tribe.

Though not so high in the social scale as the Todas, the Badagas are the most numerous and prosperous tribe in the Neilgherry hills. They number about fifteen thousand. The Todas, though a military caste, have no songs. It is not with them "the thing" to sing. When they want music they can listen to the songs and pastoral pipes of the Badagas and Kotas. The latter are a musical race. Each man has his pipe. Not the reedy assembly that makes the instrument of "the great God Pan," but a flute, with sufficiently numerous and well placed holes to render it easy to produce what may fairly be called melody. They are always ready to sing; at birth, marriage, or death.

But it is not only on such occasions that they sing. The belated traveller along hillside tracks will often hear the distant chant, the loud and sudden chorus, and then again the floating strain of the single singer, borne gently and like the reflex of some distant wave on the wings of the cool night breeze. Such echoes tell of Badaga merriment, and remind the man who is not ignorant of the brother men who dwell around him, that at that moment a whole village-full of folk are gathered round some mossy stone, listening to and then joining in the song of a rustic Homer or Badaga bard, who, neither "mute nor inglorious," leads the resounding melody. Men, women, and children are there. Ever as they sing some man or maiden springs to the front and dances to the song, light and agile as a deer or, better still, a mountaineer, such as they are. Thus with song and dance the evening glides away.

It is not certain that civilization has furnished greater nations with better modes of enjoying the silvery moonlight tide. It is quite certain that few nations can boast of better songs as far as words may go. They err in length for ears and minds polite, for one will fill an evening. They are rather songs such as the minnesingers trolled out—stories in poetry. More than ballads, less than books, they remind one, in everything but their morality and lack of appreciation of the beauties of nature, of Chaucer's stories. Imagine, if it be possible, a Wife of Bath or a Merchant's Tale that should be devoted to the wickedness of sin rather than to the pleasures of the flesh; and then in dramatic character, poetic force, vividness of colouring and completeness of story, we shall get a Badaga song.

This reminds that, as with the Canarese songs last described, a strong religious and moral thread runs through the whole. In every Dravidian tongue we see the same phenomenon. Get back to the folk literature, as distinguished from that which has its spring in

Sanscrit, that is, Brahmanic importations, and we find "the people" singing of the evils of sin, of the hideousness of hypocrisy, of the utter unworthiness of man. The sternest Judaic morality is taught with Judaic precision and force.

For want of better knowledge it has been customary of recent years to class the Dravidian tongues and peoples with the Scythians of northern Asia and eastern Russia; yet every writer who has attempted to describe the Scythic character, has placed as the fundament and key to the whole "an utter want of moral elevation," to use the words of a recent thinker. Among the Dravidians the precise opposite is the case. All who know them declare, with Dr. Caldwell, their infinite superiority in this respect to the Aryanized nations of northern India, of the valleys of the Ganges and Nerbudda.

The most prominent feature of all this class of literature is its high morality; often using very plain words and calling things by their right names, but ever preaching such truths as are, in "civilized" countries, supposed to be the peculiar property of the pulpit and very unfashionable everywhere else. Vice, as distinguished from legitimate sensual enjoyment, is never glorified in Dravidian folk songs. The more one reads them the greater is the astonishment that peoples should, in these latter days, so openly denounce the sin that is among them; should do so much to make every man, woman and child know that wickedness is evil and not good. Perhaps it is well and a mark of high civilization that all mention of evil should be taboed, except in the mouths of a privileged class; but it is surely better and a mark of noble blood, if not of higher civilization, that denunciation of evil should ring at each fireside and every village feast.

The first of the songs that follow is the funeral dirge that is sung at every cremation, a little before the actual burning. It is so beautiful, in sentiment rather than poetry, and the whole funeral ceremony is so interesting, that it will be well to look for a moment at the ritual of which the dirge forms a part.

The ceremonial commences somewhat before death. As soon as the last struggle sets in, the whole village springs into activity and earnest labor. The family gathers round the dying man. The father or senior member of the family takes a small gold coin—a remnant of times long forgotten—worth but about six pence and, therefore, very very tiny; dips it in ghee and places it in the sick man's mouth, telling him to swallow what should be his last and most important food and fortune. If the tiny coin slip down, well. He will need both gold and ghee. The one to sustain his strength in the dark journey to the river of death, the other to fee the guardian of the fairylike bridge that spans the dreaded tide. If sense remain to the wretched man he knows that now his death is nigh. Despair and the gold make recovery impossible, and there are none who have swallowed the Birianhana and yet have lived. If insensibility or deathly weakness make it impossible for the coin to pass the thorax, it is carefully bound in cloth and tied to the right arm, so that there may be nought to hinder the passage of a worthy soul into the regions of the blest.

Meanwhile, a host of men fly to every quarter of the compass. The burning must not be delayed more than twenty-four hours. The Neilgherries are large and the Badaga villages very widely scattered, so forth must go a dozen runners, speeding as if with fiery cross to call the tribe and friends of the deceased. As they run they shout in the fashion peculiar to mountaineers, so that the hills and vales for miles ring with the long drawn-out cry that seems to fly through the air like some swift dark bird, to such incredible distances does it reach. While they thus carry their news, another dozen start for the nearest shola (patch of jungle trees). With eager hands they cut off the straighter branches and hale them to the village. Another set go forth to the nearest Kotagherry (hill inhabited by Kotas), to call musicians and carpenters. The latter attack the branches brought from the shola and soon produce a pyramidal car of such dimensions as time and material permit. Others prepare bows and arrows, to show that the deceased was a warrior, and belonged to a fighting race. If the dead be a woman, a rice-pounder serves instead.

Towards evening all this is done. Then the car is covered with cloth, and the corpse is brought out on a charpoy or native cot, and laid under the car. On one side of the cot are placed the various tools employed by the deceased, his plough, his knife, &c. On the other are laid out his flute, his stick, and the bows and arrows made by the Kotas. Last of all, an empty gourd, to serve him as a drinking pot in the long journey from the known to the unknown, is laid at the dead man's feet.

With early dawn the crowd of friends comes in. Man and woman are dressed in their best. Their best is not much to be sure, except in the way of jewels, which are often very valuable. The first ceremonial is that of the dance. It begins with the male relations of the dead, who circle round the corpse, now fast, now slow, now with joined hands and then separately. Above all rises the shrill music of the Kotas, who officiate at this portion of the ceremony. Music and dance get faster and faster still. As friends arrive they join in, and with their fresh vigor keep up the frenzied round. They are supposed to be accompanying the parted soul in its rapid flight to the feet of God or, rather, to the pillar of fire, of which more will be said hereafter. The women stand around holding in their hands the emblem of their calling, a rice-beater. As the excitement rises, one or more of them will dash into the dance, whirling round and round their massive weapon. Sometimes this frantic dance will last for hours.

So far, the ceremony is much like what we know to have been common among many early races. But now commences a more solemn service which must demand the most earnest attention.

When the dance is done and the performers have

recovered breath and calmness, the nearest relations of the dead man walk in sad procession round the body. One or more of them carries a basket of rice or other food wherewith to satisfy the wandering soul or bribe away the demons or beasts who would otherwise hinder its journey. Ever as they walk one tells the goodness, the prowess, the tender care for animals, the domestic virtues of the deceased. At every fresh illustration of his manly vigor or loving heart, his parents, brothers and friends burst into fits of weeping; and what seem, and doubtless are, bitter tears of deep sorrow roll down many a sad but dingy face. Then the crowd takes up the body, its car or canopy, and all its appurtenances, and carefully places them outside the village bounds.

Again in solemn silence they stand around, until one brings within the circle a buffalo-calf. It has been carefully selected and is without blemish. One of the leading men then steps to the side of the calf, lays his hand upon its head and in a loud voice chants the dirge to which reference has been made. The lines of the poetry are so arranged that each stanza is finished by the principal verb of the sentence. The whole is a confession of sin. In the village the good deeds of the deceased were rehearsed. They stood in the presence of family and friends, and the proper rule was *nil nisi bonum de mortuis.* Now they stand before God, to whom every sin is known. Now man's unworthiness appears, and the only proper attitude is that of confession of sin. After a short invocation, the performer makes a general confession. By a conventional mode of expression the sum total of sins a man may do is said to be thirteen hundred. Admitting that the deceased has committed them all, the performer cries aloud " Stay not their flight to God's pure feet." As he closes, the whole assembly chants aloud, " Stay not their flight." The God invoked is Bassava, after whom is named the great propagator of the Vira Siva or ultra Siva worship. It is a name peculiar to Siva himself. The chief symbol of Siva is the bull *Nandi:* in Badaga the cow, *Banige.* The calf is, therefore, a peculiarly appropriate symbol, answering to the scape-goat of the Jews.

Again the performer enters into details and cries, " He killed the crawling snake, it is a sin." In a moment the last word is caught up and all the people cry, " It is a sin." As they shout the performer lays his hand upon the calf. The sin is transferred to the calf. Thus the whole catalogue is gone through in this impressive way. But this is not enough. As the last shout—" Let all be well"—dies away, the performer gives place to another, and again confession is made and all the people shout, " It is a sin." A third time is it done. Then, still in solemn silence, the calf is let loose. Like the Jewish scape-goat, it may never be used for secular work. It is sacred, bearing till death the sins of a human being.

The solemn confession done, the relatives put earth on their heads and, carrying hatchets in their hands, circle the corpse three times, weeping bitterly all the while. Lastly, they place a little earth upon the dead man's face. Then the crowd carry the body and its canopy to the nearest stream, heap up fuel round the corpse and burn the whole in one great blaze. With it are burnt jewels, cloths, implements and all the personal belongings of the deceased. While yet cremation continues, all leave the spot. Next morning the relatives return, gather up the ashes and cast them into the stream. Should any bones remain unconsumed, they are reverently placed on the ground and covered with a tumulus of such stones as the men may be able to lift. When all is over, the friends of the deceased shave their heads and faces in sign of mourning and return to their ordinary lives.

The song deserves careful attention. The version that follows is an almost literal translation, and has been drawn from a literal prose rendering which the Rev. F. Metz, the devoted and self-sacrificing missionary who has for so many years persevered in what has seemed the almost hopeless task of Christianizing the Badagas, most kindly placed at my disposal. He and his few colleagues of the Basel Mission are the only Europeans sufficiently acquainted with the Badaga tongue and people to obtain either the means or the confidence required for gaining a knowledge of the inner life of this strange people. All honor to those who have been willing to live and die among such people as the Neilgherry tribes.

DIRGE FOR THE DEAD.

Invocation
In the presence of the great Bassava,
Who sprang from Banigé the holy cow.

The dead has sinned a thousand times.
E'en all the thirteen hundred sins
That can be done by mortal men
May stain the soul that fled to-day.
Stay not their flight to God's pure feet.
Chorus—Stay not their flight.

He killed the crawling snake.
Chorus—It is a sin.

The creeping lizard slew.
It is a sin.
Also the harmless frog.
It is a sin.
Of brothers he told tales.
It is a sin.
The landmark stone he moved.
It is a sin.
Called in the Sircar's aid.*
It is a sin.
Put poison in the milk.
It is a sin.

* This is a curious example of the hatred that all Hindoo tribes felt towards the old regime. To appeal to the Rajahs or their courts was to invite oppression, to require a large outlay on bribes, to let loose false witnesses, to reveal secret mountain paths, in short, to bring upon the poor hill people all the ills that the rapacity of the governing class could inflict upon ignorant and helpless mountaineers.

To strangers straying on the hills
He offered aid but guided wrong.
Chorus.—It is a sin.

His sister's tender love he spurned,
And showed his teeth to her in rage.
It is a sin.

He dared to drain the pendent teats
Of holy cow in sacred fold.
It is a sin.

The glorious sun shone warm and bright—
He turned his back towards its beams.
It is a sin.

Ere drinking from the babbling brook
He made no bow of gratitude.
It is a sin.

His envy rose against the man
Who owned a fruitful buffalo.
It is a sin.

He bound with cords and made to plough
The budding ox too young to work.
It is a sin.

While yet his wife dwelt in his house
He lusted for a younger bride.
It is a sin.

The hungry begged—he gave no meat.
The cold asked warmth—he lent no fire.
It is a sin.

He turned relations from his door,
Yet asked unworthy strangers home.
It is a sin.

The weak and poor called for his aid,
He gave no alms, denied their woe.
It is a sin.

When caught by thorns, in useless rage
He tore his cloth from side to side.

Chorus.—It is a sin.

The father of his wife sat on the floor,
Yet he reclined on bench or couch.
It is a sin.

He cut the bund around a tank,
Set free the living water's store.
It is a sin.

Against the mother of his life
He lifted up a coward foot.
It is a sin.

What though he sinned so much,
Or that his parents sinned?
What though the sins' long score
Was thirteen hundred crimes?
O let them every one
Fly swift to Bas'vas' feet.

Chorus.—Fly swift.

The chamber dark of death
Shall open to his soul.
The sea shall rise in waves,
Surround on every side,
But yet that awful bridge,
No thicker than a thread,
Shall stand both firm and strong.
The dragon's yawning mouth
Is shut—it brings no fear.
The palaces of heaven
Throw open wide their doors.

Chorus.—Open wide their doors.

The thorny path is steep,
Yet shall his soul go safe.
The silver pillar stands
So near—he touches it.
He may approach the wall,
The golden wall of heaven.
The burning pillar's flame
Shall have no heat for him.

Chorus.—Shall have no heat.

Oh, let us never doubt
  That all his sins are gone,
That Bassava forgives.
  May it be well with him!

Chorus.—May it be well!

Let all be well with him.

Chorus.—Let all be well!

How vividly all this brings to mind the grand pictures of the Mosaic Exodus! Forget that we listen to a puny tribe of Neilgherry mountaineers, and we see Ebal and Gerizim revive; when the man of God pronounced the blessings and the curses—the good that would bring life and the ill that must cause death. No prophet was ever more explicit in declaration of sin, no people ever more ready to learn. In fact this is the grandest thing about either Ebal or the lonely village in the hills:—that a people should, in the most solemn ceremony that man can attend, with one voice denounce evil and justify the holy God, who "cannot regard sin with any degree of allowance."

More than one observer has noticed physical and facial peculiarities so strongly reminding of the Jew, that he has not hesitated to proclaim that here at last are found those lost tribes which so strangely disappeared from the world's history 2,500 years ago. These observers knew nothing of the ceremony described above. Had they known, how much louder still had been their shout of recognition. History repeats itself, and coincidence is not identity. There is nothing, positively nothing, beyond physical features and this ritual, to support the theory, and it may be allowed to pass into that great limbo where lie philosopher's stones and squared circles. Yet read the book of Leviticus, and then compare the history of the scape-goat with that of the Badaga buffalo. "He shall bring the live goat, and Aaron shall lay both his hands upon the head of the live goat, and confess over him all the iniquities of the children of Israel, and all their transgressions in all their sins, putting them upon the head of the goat, and shall send him away by the hand of a fit man into the wilderness, and the goat shall bear upon him all their iniquities, into a land not inhabited; and he shall let go the goat in the wilderness."

Is not this the exact scene that takes place each year on the Neilgherry hills? In the solemn gathering of the people, the loud rehearsing of the sin, and the still more awful reply of the great crowd, we see, combined with the touching ceremony of the scape-goat, the greatest and most solemn gathering in Judaic history after the thunders and lightnings of Sinai,—when half the people stood on Gerizim and half on Ebal. Midway stood the Levites, and one and another came forward and cried "Cursed be he that setteth light by his father and his mother." As the words left his mouth the whole multitude shouted "Amen." Even the very confession is in many points the same. The Jews said, "Cursed be he that removeth his neighbours' landmark." The people answered "Amen." Turn to the Badaga ritual. "The landmark stone he moved." The people cry "It is a sin."

Let us note a few in parallel columns.

JEWISH.	BADAGA.
1. Cursed be he that setteth light by his father and his mother.	"The father of his wife sat on the floor Yet he reclined on couch or bench. It is a sin." "Against the mother of his life He lifted up a coward foot. It is a sin."
2. Cursed be he that maketh the blind to wander out of the way.	"To strangers straying on the hills He offered aid, but guided wrong. It is a sin."
3. Thou shalt not see thy brother's ox or his ass astray and hide thyself from them. Thou shalt in any case bring them again unto thy brother.	In the song about to be quoted is the following passage describing the deeds of good men :— "When they saw on the hills the lost kine Of stranger or neighbour, they drove them all home."

Many similar parallels might be produced by running through the commands in Leviticus, but these suffice to show the remarkable coincidence in word and ritual. Yet it must be repeated that, after careful enquiry, I can discover no shadow of ground for supposing that the Badaga form has been introduced by Jewish influence, although it must be confessed that the presence in Cochin of that strange colony of "Black Jews," who distinctly claim to belong to the lost ten tribes; and the fact that Cochin is not many days' march from the Neilgherry plateau, might afford some presumptive additional evidence to the hand of the puzzled searcher. Had the Todas or Badagas been connected with the "Black Jews," the tie must have been known. On the contrary, all Neilgherry tradition points to an early journey from the north—from the great road by which every Aryan tribe entered India.

The next song is of equally interesting character. It describes the other world—"where parted spirits dwell." It is only necessary to premise that, according to Badaga belief, the soul carries with it an "eidolon" or image of its earthly body, capable of bearing pain and delighting in pleasure. The succeeding song also expresses the same idea. As another link in the great chain of evidence proving the Aryan origin of this curious literature, it should be noted that the portals of death are guarded by a gruff porter or concierge, who demands payment for permitting or aiding the passage of the departing soul. The Todas suppose that this surly keeper dwells at Makurty Peak, remarkable for the enormous precipice that forms one side. We meet this personage again and again in every Aryan race. The peculiar configuration of the Neilgherries will explain at once the idea of seeing the other world from their furthest peaks. The observer from Dodabetta, Snowdon or any other high peak, sees the low country at his feet, spread out like one vast carpet. The great distance throws a haze over the landscape that seems to render it unlike the surrounding world. The traveller who has seen Italy from the south side of the Alps will know what is meant. At one point in the Coondah range, among the Neilgherries, the wanderer sees a little cleft in the rocks that have hitherto bounded his rugged path on either side. He turns to look beyond and sees, as by a charm, that he stands on the brink of one of the most awful precipices in the world. In one sheer straight dip of several thousand feet the fascinated eye rests on the plain below. It *is* another world.

The song is a dialogue between a tender curious woman and one of the "wise men" who act as the advisers of their tribe. These wizards are greatly feared. Like the "medicine men" of the Red Indian they must be propitiated before any important work can be undertaken. Their curse brings death—their blessing commands the Gods.

THE NEXT WORLD.

Hattitippé, to see the other world,
Went walking where this sinful world of ours
Is bounded by Neilgherry rocks and steeps
Beyond Makurty Peak. Then, peering from
The furthest hill, she saw the wondrous land
Where parted spirits dwell. There came with her
Her dearest friend, to whose sad mind and eyes
Had been revealed the fate of those whose life
Had left this world to stand before its judge.
While yet she looked she thus addressed her friend:—

> "Oh brother simpleton,
> If I bend down I see
> The tails of lowing kine.
> But if I stand upright
> I see their horned heads.
> To whom do they belong?"

"No funeral rites were performed for the men
Whose cattle have come to your view.* On the earth
Their relatives died before them. So the king
Who rules in the land out of sight was their heir.
The cattle do feed in his fields—they are his."

* We see here the germs of the Hindu theory noted on page 41. The possibility of amending the condition of the dead requires that the living should never slacken in their pious labor for their ancestors—hence the monthly and annual ceremonies for the good of dead forefathers are the keystone of the whole edifice of Hindu social ritual.

" 'Tis true, my brother dear.
But now I see a tree,
And from its spreading boughs
Hang many wretched men,
Suspended by their necks.
Who then are they, I ask ?"

" Oh sister beloved, must I tell you of this,
And have your own ears never heard of the tale ?
For ever they hang from the boughs of the tree
Because they thus ended a God-given life,
And fled from the woes their own sin had provoked."

" I see a loathsome ditch
Where wretched men lie prone.
They ever seen to smoke
The brown tobacco-leaf.
Who then are these, I ask,
Dear brother simpleton ?"

" When Badagas died on the Neilgherry Hills
Their widows were robbed of the mite that was left.
The poor were oppressed by the strong and the rich.
The men that you see were great chiefs in their day,
Who grew to be rich on the spoil of the poor.
Such crimes have they done, and their punishment now
Is to lie in the ditch so defiled and unclean.
No food may they eat. To their ravening mouth
Tobacco is given. They may smoke but not eat.*
In luxury starve. In their mouths is but smoke."

* This is rather a novel pnnishment, but yet highly suggestive of the fact that luxury bought by crime is an unsatisfying thing.

"Again I see sad men,
Some garden land they bless;
Ever pouring water
On tall and gaudy plants.
Oh brother, who are they?"

"Oh sister, you surely must know about this;—
They poisoned themselves when they dwelt on the earth
With opium deadly and vile. On these hills
They ate of the fruit of this terrible plant.
So now and for ever they water the seed,
The plant and its tall swelling head. While they live
The water they pour. Thus their sin is their pain."

"But, brother, stay. I see
A narrow hill-side path,
The track of buffaloes.
In it there lies a child,
Mosquitoes cover it.
How sad and sore it cries!
Whose tender child is that?"

"The child of a woman so cruel and hard
That when, in the days of her life, a poor child,
The child of a stranger, besought her for bread,
She murmured—"This troublesome child is not mine,"
And would not receive her, nor comfort her soul.
So now, without help, her own child dies alone."

"Oh, brother, let me go
And save that helpless child.
E'en yet her lips may suck
New life from out my breast."

"Oh sister, approach not that suffering child.
The giant, with mouth like a crow, will devour
Each one that would touch that forlorn helpless babe.
All sins that are done against children on earth
Are written above, and are known at the last."

"Yet once again I see
A lovely field of grain
With ears an ell in length:
They swell as doth a pot.
Whose golden field is this?
Tell soon, oh brother dear!"

"You see the tall grain in the field of the man
Who lived to his God and did right in the world:
Who tilled his own land, and then cheerfully helped
His neighbour or friend. He gave alms to the poor,
The hungry he fed. To the cold he brought fire,
The naked he clothed, and the poor he relieved.
If now he should scatter his seed on a rock,
No barn would contain the bountiful crop."

"But, brother, now I see
Some men whose hair is smooth,
Well combed and shining bright.
One cloth around the loins
Is all the dress they wear.
Before they milk their kine
They wash in water warm.
How vast a pot they take,
And yet it fills with milk!"

"They get such abundance of white frothing milk,
Because when they saw on the hills the lost kine
Of stranger or neighbour, they drove them all home,
And saved from the tiger, the cheetah, or wolf."

" A stranger thing appears.
I see red mud out there;
And men are digging it.
Who can such wretches be?"

" These people, my sister, are those who had much
Of food and of wealth when on earth. Yet they hid
The meal they were eating when beggars drew nigh.
So now they have fallen in thick and deep mud,
From whence they may never escape. To their cries
For food and for drink, they are answered but this,—
" Eat mud, there is mud. You may drink of the mud."

" But now I see a house,
How white and clean it is!
It has verandahs wide.
Some men are writing there
Or reading, as they will.
My brother, who are they?"

" They never complained to the Sircar's dubash,*
Nor slandered their friend or their foe. In the world,
Where sins are so many, they acted aright,
And hated the rogue who could poison a foe.
God gave them their eyes, they perceived the great good,
God gave them their hands, they were used for His work,
God gave them their food, to the stranger 'twas given,
God gave them their feet, they have walked in his ways.
A happy reward is for them, they are scribes."

* Dubash is the Hindoo term for interpreter, and means—" he that speaks two languages." The dubash is an important officer in all dealings of the government with the people. See note on page 73.

"Oh brother, who are these,
Most wretched of them all?
In naked shame they're bound
To rugged gnarled trees.
They ever seem to talk,
But none are there to hear."

"Oh sister, you surely have heard who these are:—
Abandoned and profligate women, who wandered astray
From virtue and home. They have nothing wherewith
To cover their shame. They are hungry and cold."

"A new thing now I see.
Oh brother, near the road
That leadeth to the plains
A fiery pillar stands.
Beyond, a river flows.
Across, from bank to bank,
Is stretched a bridge of thread.
What can these strange things mean?"

"Look, sister, again. On the happier side
There stands a white house—the abode of the blest.
The place of the lost, where they meet their reward,
Is nearer to you—on this side of the stream?"

"Oh brother, how I wish
To reach that blissful shore!
Why did I ever come
To see such fearful things!
If, when at last I die,
A solemn gathering mourns,
And fire devours my corpse—

If toll be paid to him
Who guards the heavenly gates—
If this and more be done,
Can I obtain that bliss,
Or must I sink to hell ?"

" Alas, my dear sister, I know not of that."

What a touch of life is there in the verses that describe the lone babe! How near akin is the whole scene to that when the Great Teacher said—"Suffer little children to come unto me."—"Take heed that ye offend not one of these little ones. It were better that a millstone were tied about his neck and he be cast into the sea."

Note again the strange (to us) reverence in which the art of writing is held. To be a scribe is to enjoy the best place in heaven. No greater joy or honor can be than that one should write. As this is the summit of moral ambition, the height of physical enjoyment is to have plenty of milk, to bathe in warm water and to wear but one cloth, and that merely round the loins. The two latter point naively to the joy—warmth, that contrasts with the greatest evil the mountaineer has to meet—cold. The wearing but one cloth is an inferential not a positive good. It proves that the blessed dwell in a land so pleasant that clothing is only needed for the sake of decency, not for warmth. The water in

Neilgherry streams is certainly cold, and inability to provide either vessel or fuel for a hot bath may perhaps account for what Europeans count the greatest disfigurement of a Baḍaga, the dirt which forms so substantial a dress, in which convenience is certainly more studied than elegance.

Again we see the strong living morality of an early Aryan or Semitic people. Here is no trace of that utter lack of a high sense of right or wrong which marks the Scythian. In the deep abhorrence of suicide which gives the opium-eater and the more direct self-destroyer the worst places in hell, we mark a higher grade of thought than Latins or Greeks reached. The practice of eating opium is especially condemned. The poppy grows abundantly on the hills, and self-indulgence in the use of its juice is much too common.

How striking, too, is the analogy between our Lord's parable of the judgment and several passages of this and the preceding song. Compare Matthew—" For I was an hungred and ye gave me meat : I was thirsty and ye gave me drink : I was a stranger and ye took me in : Naked and ye clothed me : I was sick and ye visited me : I was in prison, and ye came unto me"—with the following :—

" You see the tall grain in the field of the man
Who lived to his God and did right in the world.
Who tilled his own land, and then cheerfully helped
His neighbour or friend. He gave alms to the poor,
The hungry he fed, to the cold he brought fire.
The naked he clothed, and the poor he relieved."

Also with this from the Funeral song :—

> " The hungry begged—he gave no meat.
> The cold asked warmth—he lent no fire.
> The weak and poor called for his aid,
> He gave no alms—denied their woe."

Another curious feeling that constantly oozes out is that of fear lest government should interfere in any matter concerning them. In addition to the passages given in the songs we may quote an expressive proverb, " If you appeal to the magistrate, you might as well poison your opponent's food." And again— " Riches acquired by serving the sircar (government) are like a post in a swamp, rats carry it away." " If a tiger be hungry, he will even eat grass." There was ample reason for this in the days of the petty rajahs and greater kings that preceded the English rule. While the mountain tribes were quiet and unthought of, they lived in peace. But the hungry princes needed little reminding, and an appeal for justice was but an invitation to plunder. Greedy but light-footed soldiers came close behind the bailiff along the trodden paths.

The bridge of thread reminds immediately of the Mahomedan idea of a sharp sword spanning the dreadful gulf. Some scholar with leisure and opportunity may trace the origin of this idea, and will probably light upon an interesting subject. The next song will itself explain both it and the burning pillar.

The story of Bali is a ballad. In the following rendering an attempt has been made to catch the spirit as well as the verbiage of the original. One stanza is marked as an interpolation, as it is manifestly different from all the rest of the piece. It has probably been inserted by some bard who felt strongly that opium-eating could not be too often condemned.

It is a favorite song and evokes many expressions of pity. Its form is so dramatic that the story has fair play. Other characters come on the scene only to shed light upon the heroines, and disappear when their work is done. The reader will again note with interest the purely Aryan idea of burying souls in trees, and may discover the germ of the great scheme of transmigration of souls, although there is no suspicion of the gross Brahmanic developments of the system.

STORY OF BALI.

1. A rich man lived in Marly Mund
   And daughters two had he.
   He called the twain by one strange name,
   For both should Bali be.

2. His lands were wide. Twelve yoke of kine
   Were scarce enough for tilth.
   His buffaloes were numberless,
   And golden hoards his wealth.

3. In fourteen chests the coins were hid;
They stood in one great pile.
But all his wealth could not bring joy,
His daughters were so vile.

4. The Gods looked down from heaven above—
Such sins must them provoke.
E'en they had never seen before
Such wilful sinful folk.

5. Their wrath was great, like lightning burned,
It swallowed everything.
In one short week the wealth was gone;
They stood but in their skin.

6. Where poor by hundreds once were fed,
Was not one grain of food.
Great store of gold had filled the house
Which now all empty stood.

7. The farmer prayed a wizard grey
To tell why pain so keen
And loss so great had come to him,
Who had so wealthy been.

8. The wizard said all this had come
To show that sin brought woe:
That if he wished to prosper still
His daughters twain must go.

9. The man went home and, fearing God,
His daughters from him sent.
So out into the wide lone world
The sinful women went.

10. They had not learned to earn their bread,
    In jungles food to gain.
No roof had they to shelter them
    From sun, or wind, or rain.

11. At last they reached a lofty house,
    And served there night and day.
But soon the master lost his wealth—
    Became as poor as they.

12. He asked a wizard why such wrath
    Had turned his good to bad?
He answered that a bitter curse
    Was on those women sad.

13. He sent them both away in peace,
    And looked for good again.
A plantain garden, gilt with fruit,
    Stood near to ease their pain.

14. With outstretched hands they tried to pluck
    The rich and fruity store.
The trees fell down, the fruit grew black;
    Their hunger burned yet more.

15. The gardeners saw the ruin dire
    Which round the women lay.
They called them "witch," assailed with stones,
    And hunted them away.

16. Near by there stood a Jack-tree tope,
    To it they then did run—
A cocoa-grove was just beyond—
    To both black death did come.

17. The curse was now so hard to bear,
So hot and deep their scathe,
The tears flowed down so large and fast,
The stream a bird would bathe.

18. In deep despair a tigress lean
They roused as first she fed.
For speedy death they looked and prayed,—
The tigress stared and fled.

19. " Oh, sister dear" said one of them,
" Why may we never die?
What sins so great can we have done
To merit wrath so high?"

20. " Perhaps if we would dare to go
Into a bear's dark den,
The beast may turn and rend us so
That life may leave us then."

21. They dared to go. Great stones they threw
Upon the savage beast.
In awe they wait. He turned and fled:
Rejects the proffered feast.

22. They swallowed lumps of opium
And smiled as sleep enchained.
But soon they start and vomit forth
The drug whose help they claimed.

23. With eyes close shut, nay, bound with cloth,
They rushed into a stream.
The waters parted 'neath their feet,
They stood as in a dream.

24. They hid themselves in jungle thick
    And set the grass alight.
The flames rose high, but came not near,
    Destroyed to left and right.

25. At last they chose a lofty rock
    To plunge from off its brink.
But as they stood to bid farewell,
    The rock did split and sink.

26. Most eagerly they sought for death
    In water, earth and sky.
But death would not receive their souls.
    They might not, could not die.

27. One moment more they stood and talked
    At top of some lone hill.
" No child nor husband may we have,
    So die we must and will."

28. Then casting off their little packs
    Of clothes and some few rings,
They start afresh, with vigor new,
    As seeking precious things.

29. They climbed in haste a hill so steep,
    An ox would backwards fall;
Ran quickly down the further side,
    Which would a goat appal.

30. At last they met a flock of sheep,
    By shepherds was it led.
They asked of one the way to heaven,—
    Both sheep and shepherd fled.

31. "Oh, sister dear, when we were young
We made our sins our boast.
And now sweet death denies our prayer
And heaven's road is lost."

32. Still walking on, an outcaste comes,
A tiger's skin his clothes.
He asked for food, for all they had,
Then cursed them with loud oaths.

33. "What money can we give to thee ?
We only long to die.
But tell us, outcaste, what may be
That lofty flame near by ?"

34. "The Gods have raised that flaming pile
For all men to embrace.
If but one sin remain unpurged
Death meets you face to face."

35. "Yet though to ashes you are burnt,
Hell opes that very hour.
The giant with the raven mouth
Will torture and devour."

36. "But brother, who are they we see,
Great water-pots they bear ?"
"They killed themselves with opium.
To scape all pain and care."

This verse is evidently an interpolation.

37. "Alas, my brother, where doth rest
The husband of my youth ?"
"Go ye away from me, for now
I know you both in truth."

38. " Ye are the wilful Bali folk,
    Whose sins are manifest.
  Amid Neilgherry hills ye dwelt
    And made of sin a jest."

39. Still on they went, and soon did come
    Unto that bridge of thread:
  Beside them yawned the dragon's mouth:
    In front, the pillar red.

40. By terror blanched, they stood in dread
    Of what might yet befal.
  Five angels bade them follow close,
    And on, straight on, went all.

41. The angels seized them by their throats
    And dragged them to their shame.
  " It is not large,—put both your arms
    Around that pillar's flame."

42. Beyond the stream they saw the God;
    And with him sat his wife.
  They begged the trembling women folk
    To clasp, and enter life.

43. While yet they spoke, with eager feet
    Two virgins past did run.
  Their robes were white, and bright they shone
    As either moon or sun.

44. Two bracelets glistened on one arm,
    With them a bangle vied.
  A green umbrella shaded them,
    They seemed on ghee to glide.

45. They boldly grasped the pillar's flame,
    Passed on and crossed the tide,
Fell prostrate at the feet of God,
    Who placed them at his side.

46. "Ye Gods, pray tell us who are these
    Whose garments glint with sheen?"
"The righteous daughters of good men;
    They have not walked in sin."

47. "Whoe'er is free from sinful stain
    When that his work is done,
Shall hither come and ever dwell
    Before the Holy One."

48. Then said the women to themselves—
    "If virgins such as they
Have passed the flames unhurt; then we
    Most surely can and may."

49. But ere they came to grasp the pile,
    The burning flames did dart
And seize their tender shrinking frames,
    Consuming every part.

50. Whate'er remained the angels cast
    Into the deep dark hell.
The ravening giant waited there
    And caught them as they fell.

51. He tortured them. The dragon fiend
    More bitter pains prepared.
For seven long days their pangs endured.
    So long God's wrath they shared.

52. Seven piles of wood the dragon made,
    With oil his victims drenched,
Then laid them on their dreadful bier
    Where life by fire was quenched.

53. But still the dragon's rage was hot,
    Not yet enough their dree.
The one he hid within a pig,
    The other in a tree.

54. While earth shall last they suffer thus,
    In cold or summer heat,
For none may taste or joy or rest,
    If death and sin should meet.

This sad story needs no note. It is only necessary therefore to add once more that in reading these simple but most pathetic songs, we do not meet with a single idea that is not familiar to us. The singers are a poor and almost unknown race of heathen mountaineers, far away in the extreme south of India. They repeat what is their inherited property, brought down almost unaltered from ages long passed from the history of India. No Brahman can have taught them. Even their neighbours in the plains could give nothing so pure, although presenting much in their folk-songs that is close akin. Whence did such learning, such morality come ? It partakes much of the Semitic, and much of the Aryan, but is in no sense Scythic. That the people are Dravidian, their language, their appearance, their caste system, their tradition fully prove. Recent increase of knowledge has left no shade of doubt on this point, and Caldwell admits it. If so, deep digging in Tamil and Telugu thought and literature must reveal similar ideas.

The Badaga language is rich in similar productions. The Rev. F. Metz has filled two large folio volumes with his collection of Badaga poetry. Most of the pieces are too long to come within the scope of this book, but otherwise are well worthy of public attention. They tell again and again the lesson taught so vividly in the ballads that have been quoted—that sin is an evil of which to be ashamed and for which one ought to fear;—that it is always good to do the right. It will be no slight benefit gained by this publication if it should cause scholars to persuade Mr. Metz to put the whole series before the world of letters.

While these lines are passing through the Press the Madras Government has taken action in the matter and has authorized the Commissioner of the Neilgherries, J. W. Breeks, Esq., to make an exhaustive examination of the history, religion, customs and antiquities of the Neilgherry tribes. The order does not specially mention the literature, oral of course, of the hill peoples ; but it is greatly to be hoped that this subject will be attended to. The tribes are rapidly dying out under that strange law which will not permit a ruder tribe to coexist with modern civilization. They are kindly treated and are permitted to enjoy their simple holdings, but yet decrease in number year by year. Strong drink destroys the men. The women steadily deteriorate in contact with Europeans. Children become fewer and fewer, and there seems every probability that before another century has rolled away the smaller Neilgherry races will have died out. There is no such fear in Coorg, where the people have settled on the rich wet lands and become a civilized nation rather than a rude hill tribe.

COORG SONGS.

The word Coorg is a corruption of the native name Kodagu, and belongs to the country lying on the summit of a plateau on the western Ghauts. Kodagu, from *Kodi*, means a hill, and the name as a proper noun is therefore The Hilly Country. This is by no means inapplicable, for the whole land is a series of ridges rising from the body of the Ghauts. Between the lines of hills are charming valleys, watered perfectly by the clouds from the Indian Ocean which impinge upon the Ghauts. Perennial verdure clothes every hollow and giant forest trees cover the hill slopes. Every dale is constantly receiving fresh stores of the fertilizing soil washed down from the hill sides by the monsoon rains. At the lowest point of each depression is usually some clear fresh lake, kept ever full by the constantly renewed moisture that sparkles down the rugged steeps in tiny streamlets from the cloudy summits. No wonder that the land is fertile or that its people look upon it as the most beautiful and blessed realm upon earth. They speak of it as a necklace among the countries; an image that derives especial force from the fact that, to him who views the land from the higher peaks, the many brilliant lakes lie in the sunshine on the bosom of the country in a double or treble chain of singular and brilliant beauty. The Coorg song or palamé almost invariably opens with a vivid expression of delight that Providence has given to the singers such a pleasant land. Some of these patriotic strains are worthy of more renowned countries than Coorg ever has been or will be. Let us quote a few.

Nothing higher can be seen,
Though one look through all the earth,
Than the Mahameru hill.
Brightest 'mongst the flower trees
Is the brilliant Sampigé.
So in all the fertile earth
Coorg a necklace is of gold.

One of the more modern songs contains the following glowing eulogy :

Like the star-besprinkled heaven
Are the happy Kurgi homes
On the bosom of our land.
Blooming children fill each house
Like a garth of richest flowers.
Like the royal Sampigé
Are our tall and stately men.
Strings of choicest purest pearls,
Beauteous as the forest flowers,
Are our wives and little ones.
Prosperous and well they live,
Jasmin has no sweeter smell.
E'en our cattle multiply
Many as the jungle race.
As the Cauvery river sand
So our rice and wealth increase.
None doth suffer in this land
Either want or grievous pain.
All are happy, all are rich.

Another palamé calls Coorg a

"Land of houses and of farms."

In the songs that follow other such ascriptions will be found. It is a pleasure to meet with a people so heartily and out-spokenly proud of their country. But it must be confessed that seldom has a people such reason to be proud of its national home.

This sense of material prosperity and social comfort pervades all the songs that will be quoted. It is an opposite pole of human existence to that which leads the Tamil and Canarese bards to find such sorrow in their world. Here we find no repining, no feeling of the vanity of all worldly things. Just the opposite—all is warm with prosperity, with domestic happiness, with a comfortable sense of sufficiency. Is not this very largely owing to the fact that there has not been in Coorg the same long strife between the old and new life, between Dravidianism and Brahmanism—that the people are permitted to enjoy their national hopes, to hold without dispute the old-fashioned doctrines of morality and religious right—to look into the future with the certainty that the bountiful Being who gave them their pleasant fertile land intended that they should rejoice in his gift?

The following pages will contain, besides a few children's rhymes, three of the songs that best represent the whole class. They are of considerable length—otherwise other examples might have been given. I am indebted to two earnest and capable German Missionaries, the Revs. W. Græter and George Richter, for literal translations of the originals. The first-named gentleman collected and published them in the Kodagu vernacular and also rendered most of them into English.

Mr. Richter is a striking example of the immense amount of good that one persevering, able and clear-minded man may do. Originally set down in an almost unknown country to christianize an entirely unknown people without a written literature or even an alphabet, he has by force of his high personal character obtained a first place in the confidence both of the people and its rulers. Almost single-handed he reduced the language to writing, thoroughly investigated the capabilities of the country and its people, examined and described its fauna, flora and geology.

When the people had learned to value his efforts, he opened schools and taught in them himself. So efficiently was this work done that, a few years back, the leaders of the nation came forward of their own accord to ask the Supreme Government to extend to them the school system which, in other parts of India, had only been established after years of opposition ; and only grew into vigorous life after many other years of misrepresentation, discouragement and numerous mishaps. Mr. Richter now holds the high post of Inspector of Schools and Principal of the Mercara High School—specially exempted from the operation of the rule which prohibits a missionary or clergyman from holding high office in the educational department, because, though an earnest successful missionary, there is no other man who could so command the confidence of the people. His last feat has been the production of a Gazetteer of Coorg, compiled almost entirely from the results of his own enquiries, and forming one of the best specimens of the official gazetteers which the Government of India has ordered to be drawn up in every province in India.

It is a pleasure to acknowledge that to his kindness and the literary collections of himself and his worthy colleague, Mr. Græter, I owe the originals of every one of the Coorg songs that follow. I was myself anxiously searching for them when I learned of the collection made by these gentlemen. On my application to be permitted to copy the songs, the whole were placed at my disposal, on the sole condition that Mr. Richter should possess the right of prior publication. This right has been exercised in the "Manual of Croog," where versions of the Wedding and Funeral Songs and of one of the children's rhymes have already appeared. For the present version I am responsible, except that it is necessary to state that the Funeral song is but little altered from Mr. Græter's rendering. Mr. Richter added to his other kindness by permitting me to render his literal translations into such metric form as might be thought advisable.

The series commences with the Huttari or Harvest Song. The word *Huttari* means "new rice," and the feast is the Coorgi representative of the Tamil *Pongol* or Feast of the Boiling. It is the harvest festival and corresponds exactly with the Jewish feast of Ingathering. All or almost all agricultural nations celebrate the arrival of the national food crop with great rejoicing. In the Tamil lands the key of the whole ceremony is the boiling of the first meal of the new rice. In Coorg the new rice is pounded or ground, and the flour made into a dough which is eaten by all present. With such slight variations as must have been produced by centuries of separation and by different physical circumstances the feast is of precisely the same character in all the Dravidian countries. In Malabar it is called Pudiari ; but this is the same word with Huttari, as the Tamil and Malayalim *p* becomes *h* in Canarese and Coorgi.

On the Eastern coast the paddy does not ripen till the end of the year, and the celebration takes place on the day that the sun crosses the equator to enter the tropic of Capricorn. On the West coast, around Calicut and Mangalore, the corn is ripe about the middle of September. The cultivated lands of Coorg have an elevation of about 3,500 feet above the sea, and the lower temperature retards the ripening. It happens therefore that the paddy cannot be cut in Coorg till about the middle of November, or two months later than in Malabar. It should be remembered that the word " rice" is only applicable after the grain has been cut, threshed and husked. Till it is thus ready for the table the proper name of the plant and its fruit is " paddy." This distinction should always be borne in mind. Rice is the cleaned grain. Paddy is the grain in the husk.

The learned Brahmans at Mangalore are far more ready at calculating times and seasons than the hard-working but ignorant Coorgs. It has therefore come to pass that the Coorg feast is made to depend upon that in Malabar, and happens exactly two months afterwards. Shortly before the time of the Malabar festival a messenger is sent down the ghauts to ascertain the day fixed in the lowlands. When the rejoicings have actually commenced there, he returns with the news, delivering his message to the priest of Iguttappa at the temple in the Padinalk-nad, where a small colony of Brahmans from Mangalore has settled. Here the leading men of every nad,—as each of the thirty-five divisions of the country is named—have already assembled. Then, amidst special religious services, the Coorg day is fixed, and all depart to their homes to make ready for the great occasion.

The feast occupies a week properly, but the rejoicings and holiday last for four days more. Like the Pongol it needs no Brahman. In fact its ceremonial is opposed to all Brahmanic teaching, assuming as it does that each thankful individual is able to approach the deity direct—to offer gifts and utter praise. It should also be noted that the presiding deity is the Sun, who with the rain has brought forth the golden crops.

The following description is quoted almost verbatim from that given by the Rev. G. Richter in his Manual of Coorg, and gives in a condensed form the leading portions of the ceremonial.

Six days before the chief festival of tasting the new rice, all the males, from six to sixty years, assemble on one of the Mandus of the Gráma, after sunset. The Gráma is the village. The houses do not cluster as in English villages, but stand alone on the land of the owner. But for purposes of domestic and public life all the houses in a particular valley form the Gráma or village. Mandu is the name of the open public place in which business is transacted or festive games carried on. Grámas have generally three Mandus, one called the Puncháyati-mandu for business ; a second, Dévara-mandu, on which dances are performed in the name of Bhagavati during the after-Huttari days ; a third, Uru-mandu (*i. e.*, the Mandu of the village) on which the Huttari performances take place.

The time of these national games and dances is from sunset till after ten o'clock. The whole male population of the Gráma, except little boys and old men past sixty, has religiously to attend. The assembly gathers gradually between six and seven o'clock. When the assembly is full, a space is marked out for the performances of the party. At a little distance a band of musicians, two Holeya or slave horn-blowers and two Méda-drummers, sit near a fire, which they have kindled for warming themselves and their instruments. The horns are large and of brass. The drums are a Pare (large drum) and a Kudike-pare (kettle drum of a smaller size.)

Three Coorg-men then step into the centre of the open space and call aloud three names: Ayappa!

Mahádéva! Bhagavati! The men stand in a triangle, their faces towards the centre, their backs towards the company. Ayappa is the Coorg forest-god; Mahádéva, the Shiva of the Hindus, and Bhagavati, his wife.

The Chandukutti (ball-and-peg play) now follows. The whole assembly takes part in it, the moon shedding a bright silver-light on the scene. A peg is driven into the centre of the chosen ground. A piece of rope is fastened to it by a loose loop. The people who make this preparation then seize some one, who must hold this rope. A piece of wood, generally of a creeper called Odi, is cut into seven parts, which are called Chandu, *i. e.*, balls. The man holding the rope puts six of these balls in a circle round the peg at a distance of the rope's length, the seventh is deposited close by the peg. The whole company now endeavours to pick up and carry away the balls without being touched by their guardian. The player in the centre, always keeping the rope's end in one hand, turns round and round, and tries to touch some one of the aggressors. If he succeed, the person touched must take his place and the play recommences. When six balls are abstracted, the seventh must be moved to the distance of one foot from the peg. When this also is lost, the man has to run through the whole crowd and escape, without being caught, to the musicians' place. If he reach this asylum in safety, the play is won and finished. If he be caught on his way, he is brought before the Nettle-man, an officer of the play-court, who has been waiting all the time, a long Angare-stick—a large fierce nettle—in his hand for the victim. His hands and feet are well touched and the play ends.

Now the assembly perform different kinds of plays and dances, representing the wars which in ancient times appear to have been waged between people of different districts. A man is wounded; a physician is called, who prescribes for him. Another wounded man dies, and Holeyas are called to invite his friends to the funeral. The funeral is performed. A scene of demoniacal possession is acted. Now stories are told of incredibilities. "I saw the other day a little hare attacking a tiger and breaking its neck." Reply: "Did you? I saw a buffaloe flying over the mountains," etc. Three men invoke again Ayappa, Mahádéva and Bhagavati. Dances follow, accompanied by the beating of sticks, keeping time with the music of the band outside. Feats of gymnastic strength and agility are then performed and another invocation of the three deities concludes the performance.

The Huttari takes place on the night of full moon. Early in the morning, before dawn, a quantity of Ashvatha (ficus religiosa), Kumbali and Keku (wild trees) leaves, some hundred of each for great houses, together with a piece of a creeper, called Inyoli, and some fibrous bark called Achchi, are collected and deposited in a shady place for the use of the evening. During the day, the house is cleansed, brass vessels are scoured, and everything wears the appearance of a great holiday. Beggars come and are dismissed with presents. The Méda (low caste cultivator) brings the

Huttari basket, the potter the little Huttari pot, the blacksmith a new sickle, the carpenter a new spoon, the Holeya a new mat. Each carries off his Huttari portion of rice and plantains. The astrologer follows, to communicate the exact time of the full moon, and claims his share of the Huttari bounty. The cattle are washed and scrubbed, for once; the menial servants have an extra allowance of rice; breakfast and dinner are served to the family. At sunset the whole house prepares for a hot bath.

The precedence is given to the person whom the astrologer has chosen in the morning for the ceremony of cutting the first sheaves. On his return from bathing, he repairs to the threshing floor, spreads the Huttari mat, and, while the rest are engaged in their ablutions, cuts the Inyoli creeper into small pieces, rolls each piece into an Ashvatha, a Kumbali and a Keku leaf, in the fashion of a native cheroot, and ties up the little bundle with a bit of Achchi fibre. All the bundles are placed in the Huttari basket. Now the women take a large dish, strew it with rice, and place a lighted lamp in it. This done, the whole household march towards the fields, where the silvery light of the full moon affords ample illumination. The dish with the lamp is carried in front; the sheaf-cutter follows with basket and sickle in one hand, and a bamboo bottle of fresh milk in the other. Arrived at the chosen spot, the young man binds one of the leaf scrolls from his basket to a bush of rice, and pours milk into it. He cuts an armful of rice in the neighbourhood and distributes two or three stalks to every one present. Some stalks are put into the milk-vessel. No one must touch the sheaf-cutter.

All return to the threshing floor, shouting as they walk on: "Polè, polè, Déva!" (Increase, O God!) A bundle of leaves is adorned with a stalk of rice, and fastened to the post in the centre of the threshing floor. Sufficient of the new cut rice is now threshed, cleaned and ground to provide flour enough for the dough cakes which each member of the household is to eat. The company then proceeds to the door of the house, where the mistress meets them, washes the feet of the sheaf-cutter, and presents to him, and after him to all the rest, a brass-vessel filled with milk, honey and sugar, from which each takes a draught. They move into the kitchen. The Huttari mat is spread, the brass dish, the rice sheaf, and the basket with leaf scrolls, each with a stalk of rice, are placed on it.

The sheaf-cutter now distributes the bundles to the members of the family, who disperse to bind them to everything in house and garden, doors, stools, roof, trees, etc. The primest stalk must be tied on the north-west pillar of the verandah, a sort of special offering to that point of the compass from which came up the joyous harvest as it spread to the south-east from the rich low-lands of Malabar. In the meantime the performer sits down to knead the Huttari dough of rice meal. Plantains, milk and honey, seven new rice corns, seven pieces of cocoanut, seven small pebbles, seven pieces of dry ginger, seven cardamom seeds, and seven corns of sesamum are added. Every one receives a little of this dough upon an Ashvatha leaf, and eats it. The ceremony is now over, and the sheaf-cutter mixes with the company. Supper follows, consisting of sugared rice and sweet potatoes, into which a handful of new rice is thrown, and of a substantial common repast of rice and curry. The Huttari chants resound in every house during the night.

But the Coorgs have not yet altogether done with their pleasant festival. Four after-Huttari days are added to the holy week. On the eighth day the Urukólu, or village stick-dance, collects the whole community. The women of two or three houses repair together to the Urumandu, a pair leading and a second pair following, all four beating cymbals and chanting ancient songs or impromptu verses. When they have arrived at the place of meeting, they sit down in groups with the children, and look at the dances performed by the men, who go through the evolutions of Coorg saltation, beating small rattans, of which they carry one in each hand, while they move to the time of music, which proceeds from a group of Holeyas, stationed between the assembly of the Coorgs and that of their own people, who enjoy themselves, in the same fashion as their masters, at a little distance.

Theatrical performances are added. Brahmans, Moplas, Voddas (tank-diggers from Orissa), Gadikas (snáke-dancers), Jógis (represented by little boys), play through the village.

After dinner, on the ninth day, the Nádukólu begins. This is an assembly of the whole district. Everything is done as at the Urukólu, only on a larger scale. At these assemblies, while the monotonous music plays and the large circle of dancers moves in the measured stick-dance, a couple of men from different grámas and armed with a small shield and a long rattan, step from opposite sides into the ring with a shout of defiance. Keeping time with the music, they approach and evade each other, swinging their rattans and dealing blows at the legs of the opponent and with their shield warding them off, but often the players get so excited that their single-stick sham combat ends in a mutual severe flogging, which has to be stopped by the spectators. As evening draws on the parties from the different villages separate and go home.

In the afternoon of the tenth day, the Dévarakólu (stick-dance in honor of Bhagavati) takes place in every village. The entertainment is the same as on the two preceding days. Dinners, held at different houses as appointed, terminate the feasting. On the 11th day the joyous celebration winds up with a large public dinner, that is given on some open plain in the forest, when the musicians, bards, drummers, Holeyas and Médas unite their exertions to give eclat to the festivity.

COORG HUTTARI OR HARVEST SONG.

Sun and moon the seasons make,
Rule o'er all the sky they take.
  God is Lord of heaven and earth.
All the joyous earnest toil
Happy ryots give the soil,
  Our rich land is fully worth.

Famous Jambudwipa's bounds*
Circle many fertile grounds;
  Which among them is the best?
Far above the highest hill,
Mahameru's† snows are still
  Showing where the saints are blest.

Midst the beauteous forest trees
Brightest to the eye that sees
  Is the brilliant Sampige.‡
Sweeter than the sweetest rose,
Purer than the mountain snows,
  Better than mere words may say;—

* Jambudwipa means the "island of the Jambu tree," in the cosmogony of the ancient Hindus. The universe consisted of circular continents surrounded by belts of ocean. The oceans were named according to the liquid of which they were composed—milk, ghee, water, &c. The continents were called by the name of some product. Jambudwipa includes the whole of India.

† Mahameru is the mountain of the Gods, the centre and glory of the whole cosmos. It is a mythological rendering of a physical fact, and represents the higher peaks of the Hindu Koosh, whose snowy summits are the last brilliant outlook of the fatherland from which the Aryas came.

‡ The Sampige is known to Europeans as the Champak (Michelia Champaka.) It is a noble tree with bright yellow flowers evolving a very sweet perfume. A lowland feast in the month of May is known as the Champaka Chaturdasi, the offering of these flowers being an essential part of the ritual.

Thus is Coorg the noblest land,
Rich and bright as golden band
On the neck where youth doth stay.
In this happy lovely realm
No misfortunes overwhelm.
Live and prosper while you may!

Now my friends with one accord,
Joyous on the verdant sward,
Sing we our dear country's praise.
Tell us then, from first to last,
All the wondrous glorious past,
Trolling out a hundred lays.

Like a robe of precious silk,
Green or golden, white as milk,—
Like the image in a glass,—
Bright as shines the sun at noon,
Or at night the silver moon,—
Sweet as fields with flowers and grass,—

Thus in happiness and peace,
Riches knowing no decrease,
Apparandra lived at ease.
In this glorious land he dwelt,
Forest girt as with a belt,
Coorg the blessèd, green with trees.

Soon he said within his heart,—
"Now's the time to do our part,
For the tilling of the field.
Sow we must, and speed the plough,
Dig and plant, spare no toil now,
Harvest then the ground will yield."

Thus he said, to Mysore went,
To her fairs his steps he bent,
  Where the country met the town.
Thirty-six great bulls he bought
Of the best and largest sort;
  White and black, and some red-brown.

Nandi, Mudda were one pair,
Bullocks both of beauty rare.
  Yoked together were two more;
Choma, Kicha were they called.
With them was their leader stalled,
  Kale, best among two score.

Then did Apparandra say,—
"All my bulls will useless stay,
  If I give not tools and plough."
Know ye why they worked so well?
No? Then listen as I tell
  How he made those we have now.

Choosing sago for the pole,
At the end he made a hole;
  Pushed the palm wood handle through.
Sampigè was for the share,
On its edge he placed with care,
  Iron plates to make the shoe.

Sharp as tiger's claws the nail
Fixing to the share its mail.
  Yoke and pins he made of teak.
Strongly tied the whole with cane
Strong and lithe as any chain;
  Other strings would be too weak.

When, in June, the early rain
Poured upon the earth and main,
  Sweet as honey from the bee;
All the fields became as mud,
Fit for plough and hoe and spud,
  Far as e'er the eye could see.

Then before the break of day,
Ere the cock began his say,
  Or the sun had gilt the sky,
In the morning still and calm,
Twelve stout slaves who tilled the farm,
  Roused the bullocks tethered nigh.

Six and thirty bulls they drove
Through the verdant fragrant grove,
  To the watered paddy field,
Brilliant 'neath the silver moon
As a mirror in the gloom,
  Or at noon a brazen shield.

Turning then towards the east
Apparandra gave a feast,
  Milk and rice, unto the Gods.
Then unto the rising sun
Glowing like a fire begun,
  Lifts his hands, his head he nods.

After that they yoke the bulls.
Each then other harder pulls,
  The ground they quickly plough.
Day after day the work goes on,
For the seed seven times is done,
  Then the harrow smooths the slough.

Six times more they plough the field
Before the planting drill they wield.
  This requires full thirty days.
Then a dozen blooming maids
Crowned with heavy glossy braids,
  Leave the house like happy fays.

Each one brings into the fields
An offering to the God that shields
  House and home from drought and pain.
Each one lifts her tiny hands,
Before the Sun a moment stands,
  Offers thanks for heat and rain.

Then they pluck the tender plant,
Tie in bundles laid aslant;
  Twenty bundles make a sheaf.
Next the sheaves are carried thence*
To their future residence,
  Where they spend their life so brief.

But they only plough a part
Of the field to which they cart
  Plants so tender and so young.
Just enough is done each day
For the plants they have to lay
  The new-made soil among.

* Paddy is seldom sown on the spot where it is to grow. The seed is thickly planted in a rich garden piece of the best land. This nursery is prepared with great care, as the song describes. In order to secure that its soil shall be intimately mixed with the water, the ground is ploughed no less than seven times, the trampling of the cattle being more effective than the plough. Then, to secure that the rich mud shall be of equal depth throughout, it is harrowed with a machine composed of branches of trees laid in a frame. It is only after this long preparation that the seed is laid

In the following month they weed,
Mend the bunds as they have need,
  Place new plants where others died.
Two months after this they wait
Till with corn the ears are freight
  Near the western ocean tide.

There the Huttri feast they make
For the bounteous harvest's sake.
  Spreading ever towards the east
By the Paditora ghaut,
Gilding all the land about,*
  Coorg receives the Huttri feast.

To the Padinalknad shrine
Gather all the Coorgi line,
  Offering praise and honor due.
There they learn the proper day
From the priest who serves alway
  Iguttappa Devaru.

When at last the time has come,
And the year's great work is done
  In our happy glorious land.
When the shades are growing long,
All the eager people throng
  To the pleasant village Mand.

in the mud. In a few days it comes up thick as grass on a lawn. When it is some four or five inches high it is transplanted to the field, which has meanwhile been ploughed several times. It is planted in regular lines about four inches apart. The song accurately describes the ordinary procedure.

* It has been explained how the harvest takes two months to pass from Mangalore to Coorg. It marches upwards, so to speak, by the Paditora ghaut. As we rise higher and higher the local harvest is later and later. Thus it spreads towards the east. Mangalore is on the western coast.

First they praise the God they love,
Thronèd high the world above.
  Then the Huttri games commence
And the evening glides away.
Singing, dancing, wrestling, they
  Strive for highest excellence.

When the seventh bright day begins,
Each man for his household wins
  Leaves of various sacred plants.
Five of these he ties with silk
Then provides a pot of milk,
  Ready for the festive wants.

When the evening shades draw nigh
Each the others would outvie
  In rich and splendid dress.
Thus they march with song and shout,
Music swimming all about,
  For the harvest's fruitfulness.

First they pray that God's rich grace
Still should rest upon their race.
  Waiting till the gun has roared
Milk they sprinkle, shouting gay,
Polè! Polè! Devare!
  Multiply thy mercies, Lord!

Soon the tallest stems are shorn
Of the rich and golden corn,
  Carried home with shouts and glee.
There they bind with fragrant leaves,
Hang them up beneath the eaves,
  On the north-west pillar's tree.

Then at home they drink and sing,
Each one happy as a king,
  Keeping every ancient way.
On the morrow young and old,
Dressed in robes of silk and gold,
  Crowd the green for further play.

Here they dance upon the sward,
Sing the songs of ancient bard,
  Fight with sticks in combat fierce.
All display their strength and skill
Wrestling, leaping, as they will;
  Till with night the crowds disperse.

Last of all they meet again,
Larger meed of praise to gain,
  At the district meeting place.
There before the nad they strive,
All the former joys revive,
  Adding glories to the race?

Now, my friends, my story's done.
If you're pleased my end is won,
  And your praise you'll freely give.
If I've failed, spare not to scold.
Though I'm wrong or overbold,
  Let the joyous Huttri live.

We have seen the joy of harvest. The picture will not be complete without the joy of marriage. Like most other Coorgi ceremonies it includes much feasting and physical pleasure, though not enframing a repetition of the sports which make the Huttari a sort of lesser edition of the Olympic games. The chief mover in the transaction is the Aruva or family friend,—a personage of almost unique character and position. Every Coorg house must choose its aruva from some neighbouring household. The duties of the aruva are very important, and he may be entitled the arbiter and counsellor of domestic life. Does any quarrel arise? Each party calls in his aruva and tells his tale. The aruva soothes the ruffled temper, points out the liability to error, meets the aruva of the opposite party, arranges terms of peace. Does any family difficulty spring up? Husband and wife quarrel—an unruly son disobeys his father—misfortune or error destroys the family property—in all of these and a hundred other matters the aruva is called in, the whole thing is laid before him, his counsel is asked. He looks at the matter from an impartial point of view, eliminates personal error, and decides as to the course to be pursued in every case. His decision is final and must be obeyed. To be appointed aruva to a family is to receive a public and influential token that age, experience or wisdom has changed an impulsive youth into a thoughtful worthy man. The privilege is highly prized and has, perhaps more than anything else, made the Coorg people the happy contented race we see.

The youth who wishes to marry must first ask his father's consent. This given, the aruva is called in. The ladies of the neighbourhood are then canvassed, unless the eager bridegroom have already made his choice. There need be no difficulty in ascertaining the eligibles, for every young lady who is "open to an offer" carries a few grains of paddy on her head, to show that she is able and willing to become a wife.

When this important point is settled, the aruva goes to the house of the chosen lady and announces his mission. He is immediately referred to the aruva of the lady's family, with whom the matter is discussed. If the lady and her family be willing, the first sign of the happy event consists in the careful sweeping of the house of the bride. Then a brilliant lamp is lighted in the house verandah, and the aruvas, supported by the head of each house, stand face to face under the lamp. Now the man's aruva solemnly asks of his fellow the hand of the young woman. The bride's aruva agrees, and asks for some token of the engagement. He receives a coin or other valuable gift. Then the two aruvas and the two fathers shake hands. The light above them represents the Sun-god, and is the binding witness of the agreement.

The young people are now betrothed. The marriage need not take place at once, and seldom does. The girl, if not already arrived at the age of sixteen, must wait till she has. But even if this be not the case, the betrothal usually takes place amid the glad times of Huttari; while the marriage will not occur till April or

May, when the hot season has made the earth hard as the nether millstone and utterly unworkable.

In the latter days of March the astrologer is consulted. He must fix upon a lucky day. This done, ten days before the event the aruvas send out invitations to the relatives of their respective houses. The actual family sit idle while the relatives, under the control of the aruva, make all preparations that they deem fitting. Many an avaricious man grieves over his melting stores and diminished riches, but is utterly unable to check what he deems such reckless profusion. His keys are not his own during these dreadful ten days. On the day before the marriage every household in the valley is asked, and as the sun sets at least one man and one woman from every house must appear, else it will be presumed that some deadly hatred parts the families. With this large accession of labor the work grows apace. Great sheds of palmyra or sago leaves are erected to cover the festive boards or rather grounds—for tables are out of the question. Pigs, the chief element of a feast where it is mortal sin to eat beef, are killed by threes and fours. Rice is boiled in the largest vessels that can be procured. Everything portends a valiant eating. All is ready by the dark hours and then relatives and friends reward themselves by enjoying the first dinner of the series.

With early morn of the next, the great day, all are astir again. In each house a crowd of eager but clumsy friends surrounds the happy man or woman. Both bride and bridegroom must be bathed, dressed, perfumed, bejewelled and made altogether as uncomfortable as human nature can permit. Those who cannot get near the principal personages busy themselves with the property of the pair. Still more pigs are killed, cut up and set up before the fire. Boiling rice steams from the courtyard. Plantains lie about in heaps. Then they wait for the lucky hour.

When the moment arrives, the bride and bridegroom, each in their own family house, are led to a sort of throne prepared for the occasion. The relatives and friends form in line in order of dignity or relationship. In a long procession they defile before the bride or bridegroom as the case may be, for as yet the pair have not met. Each one, as he passes, drops a few grains of rice on the head of the unfortunate bride or her betrothed. Each one pours a little milk into his or her upturned mouth. Each one gives a present of a few annas. When the long file has passed, the victim is led into a dark inner room and there receives renewed congratulations. Soon, however, the appetizing perfume of roast pork distracts the attention of the guests, and they turn away to the feast. As they eat, the bards sing the song that appears on the next page but one, and such others as may appear suitable. If the house be wealthy, an improvisatore will be engaged to sound the praise of each guest before his face.

When the sun bends towards the west, the bridegroom sets out for the house of the bride, surrounded by all his relatives and guests. Singing and music accompany them. The walk aids digestion, and much is it needed. No sooner does the procession arrive than a new feast is set out, of which all must partake. The merriment is greatly aided by an abundant supply of ardent spirits, of which the Coorgis are somewhat too fond.

But in the nature of things eating must come to an end, or at all events must have some moments of intermission. Advantage is taken of this interval to perform the actual binding ceremony. The friends and family of each party draw up in line facing each other. Between the rows a lighted lamp is placed, to symbolize the sun. Then the bride's aruva steps forward and loudly asks—"Do you give to our daughter, house and yard, field and jungle, gold and silver?" The bridegroom's aruva steps forward and says, "We do." Three times is the question put and answered. When the agreement is thus concluded, the bridegroom's aruva takes three pebbles and gives them to the bride. She ties them in the hem of her cloth to show that thus she has received the ownership of her husband's house and land.

She is then led into her father's kitchen and placed upon a chair. Again a lamp is lighted, and the bridegroom comes in. He puts a few grains of rice on her head, pours a little milk in her mouth and gives her a little money. His party passes by in single file, paying her the same honors and openly accepting her as a member of their family. When all is done, the new husband takes his wife's hand and leads her into the outer room. Here she bids farewell to her relatives and friends and departs to her new home. All the party follow her and find a new feast, the third since noon, ready for them. Again they eat, and again the bards sing. When satiated nature can feast no longer, the bridegroom's aruva leads him and his wife to their own room and the ceremony concludes.

WEDDING SONG.

For ever rule, for ever live,
Almighty God, our king and Lord.
Our sovereign be, protection give.

Though Coorg is but a tiny land,
It shineth like a pearly band
Across the bosom of the earth.
Twelve valleys lie within its girth,
And thirty-five bright nads there are.
Amidst the whole the brightest far
Is that in which for aye doth bloom
A heavenly flower, whose rich perfume
Has published Apparandra's name.
And from this house a great man came.

Mandanna was a mighty man
Whose fame throughout the country ran.
For when he asked his Lord for land
The king could not his wish withstand,

But gave, without a price or fee,
  The richest land his eyes could see.*
Then with his wealth he bought a band
  Of Holeyas† to till his land.
He purchased next at prices great
  Sufficient bulls for his estate,—
To plough the field and drag the wain,
  To house the corn and tread the grain.
With this Mandanna's toils were done
  And ease and comfort fully won.

But though he was a mighty man
  Mandanna would the future scan.
For constantly this one idea
  Would fill his mind and haunt his ear:—
"Much rice have I and costly dress,
  But none to clothe or souls to bless.
With precious stones my chests are rife,—
  A useless heap when I've no wife.
And all my toil is toil in vain
  Unless a child the house contain.
For no! There is no joy on earth
  Without a wife or children's mirth.
The tank that never gathers rain
  Was surely dug and built in vain.

* The richness of land depends almost entirely upon the quantity of water that is available for cultivation. In the original the grant is called "jumma" land or freehold. This tenure is called in Malabar "jemm."

† Holeyas were prædial slaves until the British conquest. Slavery and the slave trade were things of every day life on the Western Coast till recent years, and it is said that, even now, there are thousands of persons living as slaves simply because they know not they are free.

Of little use is garden fair
  Unless the flowers flourish there.
For who would like to eat cold rice
  Unless some curds should make it nice.
So every house should have a son,
  And little children in each room."

With thoughts like these within his heart
  He needs must act a manly part.
So on a lovely Sunday morn,
  The dew yet sparkling on the corn,
He took his meal, put on his best,
  Then lifted up his hands and blessed
The God who through all time had cared
  For him and those whose love he shared.
His sturdy staff with silvered bend,
  His aruva and trusted friend,
Were all the company he took
  When he his house and home forsook
To seek through hill and dale a wife.
  Through weary weeks of anxious life
He wandered all the land about,
  Until his shoes were quite worn out.
He sat and pondered on each green
  Until his clothes were torn and thin.
So long he journeyed in the sun
  His reeling brain was quite undone.
And e'en his stick grew much too short
  Although at first too long 'twas thought.

In every place the mighty man
  Sought high and low, through every clan,
A girl who would be good and kind.
  At first no house would suit his mind.

Perchance the house was good enough,
  But there the servants were too rough.
The servants might not be such fools,
  But then he did not like the bulls.
The bulls were sometimes large and strong,
  But then the lands were all tilled wrong.
The culture perhaps could be set right,
  The pastures then were poor and light.
If all his carpings were in vain
  The maid herself was very plain.

At last he heard some joyful news,
  And hope his mind could not refuse
Repaid his pains to bear so hard.
  There livèd in the Nalkunad,
In Pattamada's house and care,
  A maid of grace and beauty rare.
The maiden's name was Chinnawa.
  When great Mandanna heard of her,
The aruva and he set out
  And slowly, like two men in doubt,
Proceeded to the house, and sat
  Upon the pyall,* where a mat
Was placed beneath the leafy shade.
  When Chinnawa, the lovely maid,

* Almost every house in Southern India has a sort of bench, made of brick and mortar, extending along the whole front of the house against the main wall. This bench or pyall is usually about two and a half feet high and three feet broad. It is the first reception place of all visitors or strangers. The laws of caste make it necessary; for, otherwise, the cultivator might receive into his house a low caste trader or messenger who would pollute the whole house. The pyall is outside the house and, by a convenient custom, cannot be polluted. Hence every stranger must halt here until his business and caste are known. In the hot weather the males of the family sleep on the pyall.

Was told that weary men from far
Were come to them, she brought a jar
Of water, poured it forth for them.
And next she brought a mat with hem
Of gold, for them to sit upon.
Then at the door she waited long.

"My friend," she asked, "Why take you not
The water from the silver pot?
Pray use it, and then call for more."

"I will, my dear one, and will pour
It on my feet, if always thou
Wilt give it as thou gav'st it now."

She answered, "If you come each day
The water I will give alway."

"To-morrow I will come again,"
Mandanna thought, and so did deign
To wash his feet and hands and face.
Then, seated in the highest place,
Mandanna said unto the maid
"My pretty maiden, give thy aid
And tell where doth thy father stay."

Then she—"My father went this day
To join a meeting on the green,"

"And where then hath thy mother been?"

"She went to grace a wedding feast
At potter's village towards the east."

"Your brother, is he not within?"

"My brother took his bulls to win
A load of salt from down the ghaut."*

An hour or two were passed in thought
  Before the father could return.
Mandanna's heart towards him did yearn;
  He bowed and touched the old man's feet.
Another hour or two they wait,
  And then the mother homeward came.
Mandanna bowed before the dame.
  Once more an hour or two pass by
And then the brother cometh nigh.
  To him Mandanna lowly bowed.
And now, in eager converse loud,
  They talk about their friends and kin.
"Oh cousin dear" they all begin,
  "We wish so much you'd let us know
For why you on your travels go?"

  "My dearest father, I have heard
Amongst the bullocks of your herd
  Are many that you wish to sell.
'Tis also said, I trust it well,
  A lovely maiden dwelleth here
Of age to wed this very year."

  "Last month the bullocks were all sold.
Two months before, a suitor bold
  Was wedded to the lovely maid."

* The word ghaut is used in Southern India to express a mountain pass. Thus the road from the plains to Ootacamund is called the Coonoor ghaut. The British Government has converted many of them into splendid roads.

To this Mandanna answer made—
  "Let those who went be as they will,
Give her to me that's maiden still."

Again the grey old farmer spoke—
  "Why did you say before these folk
That I your dearest father am ?"

Then wisely said that mighty man—
  "Your lovely daughter I admire,
And hence I count you as my sire.
  The stately palm, when once 'tis seen,
Demands our ardent praise, I ween.
  But we forget to look once more
Upon a tree both old and poor."

Again the father spoke and said—
  "I give to thee my dearest maid.
If you will take her, give a pledge."

"Shake hands with me. I do allege
  Before these men that I will wed
The lovely maid," Mandanna said.
  "And as a pledge I give this coin."

And now with one accord they join,
  Preparing for the marriage feast.
The father called the aged priest,
  The women swept in merry mood,
The stores were filled with luscious food,
  And all was ready for the night.
Then, where the beauteous brazen light
  Hung from the ceiling's wooden beam,
The aruvas and friends did stream
  From both the houses of the pair,

Betrothal rites to see and share,
  And fix the lucky wedding day.
The bridegroom gave his blushing fay
  A necklace all of yellow gold.
And, waiting till away had rolled
  Eight slow-gone days and sleepless nights,
Claimed from his bride a husband's rights.

The two very interesting songs that have preceded this have occupied so much space that it is not possible to describe at length the funeral ceremonies. They have gradually approximated to the ordinary Hindoo fashion, and do not deserve particular attention, except in regard to the strangely beautiful song which forms the most touching part of the service. Its pathos and imaginative power are very marked. It is strange that all the Dravidian nations should have first created and then preserved such fine lyrics for occasions of cremation or burial. The ritual has fallen completely into the lowland rut, but the song retains its pristine vigor and popular acceptance. It would seem as if the mind set up a sort of barrier against sacerdotal influence in certain points,—reserving them, as it were, as perpetual tokens of early independence. The Pongol festival among the Tamils, the Sankranti among the Canarese, the Pudiari of Malabar and the Huttari of Coorg, are other instances standing out from the ordinary dead level, like the droogs or hill forts on the Carnatic plain,—landmarks showing the way back towards ancient life.

FUNERAL SONG.

Woe! My father, thou art gone!
Woe is me! For ever gone!
Gone with all thy virtuous soul!
How, my father, can I live?
Woe! Thy days are ended now,
And the share, assigned to thee
By the Lord, is all consumed
And no further portion given.
Oh! Thou didst not wish to die,
But to stay among thy folk.
Surely man came to this world
But to die; not one of us
Is exempted from this doom.
Onward, onward roll the years;
Oh! How soon were thine cut off!
Like the eagle in the sky
Thou wast roaming here on earth.
Woe! The string of choicest pearls
Round the neck of favored child
Is for ever burst and lost!
Woe! The clear and brilliant glass,
Fallen from our trembling hands,
Fallen broken to the ground!
Woe! The wrath of God most high,
Floods of fiery mighty wrath,
Beating on the lofty hills,
Swept their summit to the ground!
Like our enemies at night,
Breaking into peaceful homes,
Slaying all the valiant men;—
Even thus the mighty God

Suddenly cut off thy days.
Like the top of Tumbemale
In the summer sultry noon,
When the sun is burning hot,
And the grass is set on fire :—
Thus, O father, was this house
Desolated by thy death !
As the raging storms in June
Break the fruitful plantain trees
In the garden round our house :—
Thus, O father, didst thou die.
When the floods destroy the shed,
Where the stores of wood are hid,
All the house is in distress.
When the meeting hall falls down,
All the villagers lament.
If the temple be destroyed,
All the land is full of grief.
Thus our house is sore distressed
By our father's sudden death.
As they quench the shining flame
Of the beauteous golden lamp,
Thus has God destroyed thy life !
As the stately Banyan tree
In the lofty mountain grove,
Which the ax has never touched,
Is uprooted by the wind ;—
Like the bright and shining leaf
Of the royal Sampigé,
Broken from the stem and dead ;—
Thus, O father, didst thou die !
In the days of life thy hand
Hast upheld and fed our house.
Thou hast planted all our fields.

Thou hast laid the corner-stone,
And our lofty house hast built
To the roof, with costly beams.
Thou hast built the solid gate,
And the courts around the house.
Oh ! my father, yesterday
Fallen sick upon the bed;
And to-day before the feet
Of the Lord of heaven and earth :
And to-morrow, like the sun
Setting in the cloudy sky,
Thou shalt sink into the grave:
Woe ! my father, thou art gone !
Woe ! my father, ever gone !

Many persons will note with pleasure the nursery rhymes of the Coorgs, reminding, as they do so pleasantly, of the children's poetry of our own land. Considerable effort has been expended in the vain attempt to gather such songs in all the Dravidian tongues. They are sung only by the women, and are never written down. But a Hindoo woman has an insuperable objection to permitting a European to know aught of the internal economy of her house. The secrecy of domestic life, to which Sir H. S. Maine in his "Village Communities," draws marked attention, forbids that a stranger should ever be informed of anything so private as the mode in which a mother soothes her child to rest. I have heard women thus singing again and again, but when they are asked to repeat for our information what they have told the child, they pretend not to understand what we mean or, if this be impossible, declare that they have forgotten the rhymes. There is a favorite Tamil nursery song of considerable length, portions of which have been obtained, but it is better to wait till further patience and kindness draw it forth in its entirety than to publish isolated portions that would give little idea of the merits of the whole piece.

Of course, no Hindoo would be so rude as directly to refuse a request made by a superior. Politeness and presumed necessity are satisfied by the invention of a string of excuses, which generally cause the impatient European to turn away with the exclamation—"What liars these people are!" He does not care to think that the people are bothering their brains to discover the best way of avoiding the rudeness the European would drive them to. Such points of etiquette are small things but are great obstacles, preventing much social intercourse.

All the Hindoo children's songs are alliterative. Some carry the jingle to an extreme, reminding of the famous English lines beginning with

"Peter Piper picked a peck of pepper."

The fifth of the songs that follow is a good example of this. It begins thus,

Chemb chemb chemb yedet,
Chembanda mandi duddi yedet,
Manika mand mani yedet.

The alliteration is largely caused by the use of words of the same or nearly similar spelling but of entirely different meaning. As if we should say—

"A bear was bearing a bare bugbear."

Take for example the last of the three lines given above,—

Manika mand mani yedet.

The first word, *Manika,* is a proper name. The second, *mand,* abbreviated from *mandi* or *nandi,* means a bull. The third, *mani,* is the word for a bell. So in the first line, the second *chemb,* abbreviated from *chembu,* means a brass water pot ; while the first is a proper name. In the fourth song the same thing appears very plainly. Benga is the name of a place, but the Coorgi word for to praise is also *benga.* So, in the last line, the Coorgi word for stop is also *benga.* The second line in the original is " Páditobb páduva," where the word *padu* means in the first instance a place and, in the second, the verb to sing. The form is so curious that we may quote another from the first song. This in the original opens thus :—

Kāk, kákéka!
Kákera mangale kek.

Here the first word, *kāk,* is the imperative of to call. The second, *kákéka,* is a compound word, *kak* meaning crow, and *eka* meaning sister ; and the whole is—

Call the crow's sister.

In the second line, *kák,* in the word *kakera,* still means crow, but the last word, *kék,* is the questioning adverb of time, *when.*

The songs also indulge in frequent imitation of natural sounds. We may refer again to the second set of lines. They run in the original something like this,—

Chakke kari
Chada, chada, béva.
Kambala kari
Guda, guda, béva.

We may render then closely as follows :

When the fruit of jack-tree boils,
It singeth—" chada," " chada."
When the kambala fruit boils,
It singeth—" guda," " guda."

The words chada and guda mark very distinctly the different sounds caused by the breaking of the bubbles that rise from liquids of different density when boiling. So in the next song the word we render by " cooing" is in the Coorgi " *kuthru,*" with the *r* pronounced very softly, giving a better representation of the dove's note than even our own word.

It is much to be desired that competent hands should follow up this branch of the subject, as it has often been found in other countries that such domestic literature preserves the most ancient ideas and those most valuable in tracing national relationship. As a curious illustration it may be mentioned that " pussy," the English domestic word for cat, appears in the Dravidian languages almost unaltered as " pusei," a cat.

CHILDREN'S RHYMES.

THE CROW'S WEDDING.

Call the crow's sister!
When is the wedding?
To-morrow or Sunday morn.
All the kite's young ones
Perished in the stream.
All the crow's young ones
Are searching for cheese.

THE BOILING.

When the fruit of Jack tree boils,
It singeth "chada," "chada."
When the kambala fruit boils,
It singeth "guda," "guda."

THE DOVE'S FAMILY.

Cooing, cooing, cooing dove!
How many young ones have you?
Five little ones I have hatched.
Where are the little ones now?
On a strong bough I left them.
I cannot see them on the bough,
A crow has carried them off.

RAIN.

While Benga praises thee,
And Padi sings to thee,
Stop, rain, stop!

This song may perhaps be better rendered thus :—

While Benga belauds thee,
And Padi sings padas,
Stop, rain, stop !

TAKINGS.

One Chemba took a brass pot,
And Chemba's wife a tom-tom,
The bull takes up a bell.
Young Kapla took a horn
And Eyappa a stick.
The girl must have a cloth,
And I a spoon of flour.

The next two songs, about the fingers, will immediately strike a well remembered note in the memory. Who has not heard a thousand times—

This pig went to market,
This pig staid at home,
This pig had roast beef,
This pig had none,
And this one cried, "pee-wee !"

It is an almost exact reproduction of the idea of the following song, which has never before been heard beyond the confines of Coorg. Both songs are accompanied by the same action—the mother or nurse pulling each tiny finger as she refers to it in the song. Have they not come out of the same nursery ?

THE FINGERS.

The little finger nail is small,
The finger for the ring is gold,
The middle finger loveth coins,
The fourth is calléd Kotera,
The thumb is Mùrutìka,
And both are gone for cheese.

THE TEN FINGERS.

Count the little fingers and those that bear the ring,
Middle fingers, forefingers and the thumbs are ten.

The following is very familiar, but I cannot call to mind the home lines, and a foreign station does not afford the help that the English student finds so ready to his hand.

LITTLE CHICKENS.

An old story, an old story !
Clever Brahman, an old story !
What shall I say ?
I know none.
Little chickens ! little chickens !
Sing me a song !
What can I sing ?
Pyong ! Pyong !

COLORS.

The mother is black,
The daughter is white,
And the grand-daughter is like gold !

The birth of a child (again quoting from Richter's Manual) renders not only the mother of the new born babe, but the whole house unclean, and equally pollutes every one who may come in contact with them. This ceremonial uncleanness (Sútaka) lasts for seven days, be the babe male or female. The mother is confined for two months to the house and is not expected to engage in any work, but to recover her strength and to devote herself entirely to her child. This singular custom no doubt greatly contributes to the general good health and vigour of the Coorg women. Daughters are not much valued. They must be brought up, and yet are destined to be entirely alienated from the house by their marriage. Boys are the stay of families. As soon as a Coorg boy is born, a little bow made of a branch of the castor-oil plant, with an arrow made of a leafstalk of the same plant, is put into his little hands, and a gun fired at the same time in the yard. He is thus, while taking his first breath, introduced into the world as a future huntsman and warrior. This ceremony, however, has almost lost its meaning and ceases to be generally observed. On the twelfth day after birth, the child is laid in the cradle by the mother or grandmother, who on this occasion gives the name, which in many instances is both well-sounding and significant : thus for boys—Belliappa (silver-father), Ponnappa (gold-father), Mandanna (the brother of the village-green) ; for girls—Púvakka (flower-sister), Muttakka (pearl-sister), Chinnawa (gold-mother.)

The cradle, woven of slit bamboos and cane, and fitted to be hung up for swinging, requires but a little trimming to render it as tidy as any fashionable berceaunette ; at all events the little Kódagu smiles and sleeps in it as happy as a prince. As his mother bends over her darling her overflowing love and happiness find vent in the Coorg lullaby :—

Júwa, júwa, baby dear !
When the baby's mother comes,
She will give her darling milk.

Júwa, júwa, baby dear !
When the baby's father comes,
He will bring a cocoanut.

Júwa, júwa, baby dear !
When the baby's brother comes,
He will bring a little bird.

Júwa, júwa, baby dear !
When the baby's sister comes,
She will bring a dish of rice.

TAMIL SONGS.

At the extreme of the social scale farthest removed from the hill tribes is the great Tamil nation. It occupies the country from the Mysore plateau on the north to the sea on the south, and is constantly extending its possessions in Ceylon, first impoverishing and then expelling the Cingalese. Twenty millions of persons speak the Tamil language and form the most intelligent and civilized nation south of the Ganges. With the intellectual power of the Bengali, they combine much of the physical energy of the Mahratta, and the literary culture of the Hindi. Never having been overwhelmed by Mahommedan invaders from the North, they preserve, almost intact, the national characteristics of ages that have long passed from memory in the Gangetic valley, and there is probably no district in India that more faithfully represents Hindoo life before the inroads of the Affghan Mahmouds, than the quiet villages of Tanjore, round Combaconum and Manargudi.

As the Tamils thus lead the Dravidian nations, it has

seemed right to describe their folk-literature at greater length and over a larger area. The better classes are especially fond of the Adwaita* songs that will come first. At the other extreme are the purely laboring tribes, known to Europeans under the common name of coolies. The strains to which they labor are well worthy of notice. Those that follow were taken down on the spot, as they were sung by a number of coolies who were at work driving piles. Between these extremes and common to all classes except the lowest, are the songs or, to speak more correctly, the chapters of the Cural, which is as truly the national representative of Dravidian people's literature as Homer was of the Greek.

The Adwaita philosophy teaches that the deity is the one great essence, filling all space and time. It is separated by a very narrow line from pantheism, and it will be noticed that some of the expressions employed have slipped into pantheism. "Everything is of God" is the exact maxim; and it is no wonder that the masses should render it without the particle, and say "Everything is God."

The impossibility of ensuring that the many shall catch and retain a fine intellectual distinction has led to another set of expressions that will startle the reader. Adwaita teachers say, "Since everything is of God, it must have some good purpose or, to speak more accurately, some divine purpose. Therefore we must call nothing that the world contains good or bad.

* For a description of the Adwaita philosophy, see page 3.

It may seem strange to us, but God is greater than we, and knows all about it." This is not far wrong, but was very easily carried on into the expression "Whatever I chose to do is good."

The teachers say again, "See God in everything, and therefore be just, be without fear and equally without desire. Nothing you ought to have is withheld, and therefore hope or desire nothing. Nothing can hurt unless God wish it, therefore fear nothing." For this some are quite ready to say, "Have neither hope nor fear, therefore nothing is wrong,—virtue and vice are terms without meaning." Notwithstanding this misconception, there need be no hesitation in asserting that the tone of the songs is highly moral, and that the oneness of God is as strongly maintained as by any Christian.

What will demand even more attention is the palpable contradiction given by the songs to what we are accustomed to call Hinduism. If they be, as in fact they are, the correct expression of the views of the mass of the Tamil people of the better class in the Madras Presidency, we are compelled to admit that the Dravidian peoples differ largely in their religious ideas from their northern brethren, and that such doctrines could not have come out of the system which presents Krishna and Kali, Rama and Hanuman as the greatest objects of worship, and their deeds as true specimens of the conduct of the deities who rule heaven and earth. It is commonly said that the Adwaita philosophy is a Brahmanic development, like the Sankhya and Nyaya systems of northern India. To some extent this is true ; but only in this, that the learned Brahmans carried on into scientific definition and scholastic shape the principles they found so firmly fixed in the Dravidian mind that they had to choose between accepting the principles or forfeiting their own influence. The indigenous Dravidian existence of the ideas that lie at the root of the Adwaita philosophy is proved by the fact that all the early Dravidian literature is of the like character, and it is never pretended that this great series is otherwise than pure Dravidian; not only independent of, but opposed to Brahmanic influence.

After the Adwaita songs are purposely inserted some very popular songs by Kapila, Sivavakyer and other very early Dravidian (Tamil) writers. The most cursory comparison will show that one spirit breathes in all. Nor will it be difficult to see how the later philosophical songs have grown out of the earlier outbursts of passion and deep feeling. There is also added an abstract of the Tiruvalluva Charitra, valuable both for its evidence that even the Brahmans acknowledge that the early Tamil literature was not dependent on Sanscrit, and also for the further witness it gives as to the ideas of religion and the Godhead that were current in very early times.

The profoundly religious spirit that pervades every member of the series will seem so strange that many will ask whether these songs are fair samples of a great mass or mere sporadic efforts of some great men who rose above their fellows. It is therefore distinctly asserted that they are fair samples of a great national literature. If any reader will take the trouble to study that great magazine of early Tamil literature—Ellis' Cural, he will find a thousand examples of similar character. It is strictly true that every one of the songs given below is popular in the most rigid sense.

The thoughtful reader will find much in Sir H. S. Maine's "Village Communities" and especially in the second lecture, to show how it has become possible that the acknowledged written literature should be saturated with sacredotalism and entirely devoted to the interests of the Brahmans, and yet that this should not represent the views and feelings of the masses, whose true voice is only seen in that literature which is not written and thereby withdrawn from the influence of the educated literary caste. It is superfluous to repeat what Sir H. S. Maine has so well exhibited, and I would only quote one passage bearing on the very question of the songs. He says of the people of India as distinguished from the Brahmans—"Those who know most of them assert that their religious belief is kept alive not by direct teaching, but by the constant recitation in the vernacular of parts of their sacred poems."

We begin with a dialogue between Rama and Vasishtha, the famous rishi. It is noticeable from the fact that the deity seeks information from the rishi, and would seem to teach that, in the mind of the Tamil writer of the song, Rama is rather the historical hero than the Puranic incarnation of Vishnu. This may not be the case, however, as a similar application from gods to men for advice is not uncommon in more polished literature. Vasishtha is the Vedic priest. The writer in quoting him appeals from Philip drunk to Philip sober, from modern Brahmanism to the ancient Vedas.

It remains only to make a last note, that, in the Adwaita system, true worship is supposed to be begun by what Methodists would call a "conversion,"—a change from darkness to light. This change introduces the state of "knowing." Before it, a man knows nothing of God, he can even worship a stone. After it, he perceives the essence that fills all things, and "knows" that God is, and is so filled with this knowledge that nothing else can claim a moment's thought. This very curious fact deserves the more attention because the conversion is not accompanied by or dependent upon any initiatory rite, like those of the later Greek sects. The change does not come because of a flood of new light thrown upon the mind from without, as by the instruction of a teacher or the performance of mystic rites. The enlightenment which causes the great change of nature comes from within. It is as if some veil or shutter within the soul is suddenly raised, so that the mind can at once look right at God and thereby learn what He really is. The devotee did not *know* before because he could not see. Now the obstacle is removed. He can see and therefore "knows."

TAMIL ADWAITA SONGS.

GOD IS A SPIRIT.

Vasishtha! Rama speaks to thee and asks—
Where may a sinner find those holy things
That drive out, root and branch, each fault and sin,
And give to him who worships perfect peace?

To him Vasishtha. God, supreme and great,
Dwells not in mortal flesh, nor hath He frame
Of substance elemental. He is not
Confined in what the simple call a God—
In Hari, Hara,* and the minor host.
The Godhead is not even mind itself:
'Tis He, the Uncreate, who knoweth all,
Who ne'er began and never hath an end.

Rama.

But will that God bow down and dwell with men,
Abide in things that have no worth or praise,
That are not one, but some and separate?

Vasishtha.

He hath no end nor had beginning. He
Is one, inseparate. To Him alone
Should mortals offer praise and prayer. Poor fools
Must bow to idols—they cannot discern
The higher things. As when some weakly man,
Who cannot walk a mile, is urged to pace

* Hari and Hara are terms for Vishnu and Siva respectively, and have previously been explained. See page 44, note.

Such distance as he can,—so fools adore
An image. Not to them the perfect bliss
Of knowing inner things. The wise man saith
That God, the omniscient Essence, fills all space
And time. He cannot die or end. In Him
All things exist. There is no God but He.
If thou wouldst worship in the noblest way
Bring flowers in thy hand. Their names are these:
Contentment, Justice, Wisdom. Offer them
To that great Essence—then thou servest God.
No stone can image God—to bow to it
Is not to worship. Outward rites cannot
Avail to compass that reward of bliss
That true devotion gives to those who *know.*

How strange that idolatry should flourish most by the side of such teaching ! One is never tired of noting the marvellous contradiction given by this literature to our commonly received notions. If the contrast should seem to be marked too often, it is because every new song that has been brought to light has more vividly expressed the difference between the real feelings of the people and those which have so uniformly been ascribed to them. Long and familiar intercourse with natives must lead every one who can look below the surface of the life around him to expect much that is opposed to idolatry and the Puranic absurdities. But the great mass of these poems go beyond what ordinary conversation usually sets forth. This proves, what might perhaps have been foreseen, that the influence of the sacerdotal caste has caused even those who love the doctrines of their ancestors to modify them sufficiently to be able to use them in combination with more fashionable ideas. The Brahmans are at the top of the social ladder, and their position is strengthened by the fossilizing influence of our policy. They therefore set the tone of educated life. Sumner Maine also notes this. His second lecture on Village Communities is full of striking thoughts, explaining why English supremacy has very efficiently though unintentionally contributed to strengthen the sacerdotal influence, killing popular tradition by the weight of Brahmanic written law.

If the people have gone towards the Brahmans, the reverse process has not been less marked. It is probably owing to the steady approach of the higher Brahmans towards Dravidian monotheism that there is now so great a gulf between them and the temple and domestic priests. The purohita is looked down upon as an ignorant servant of unreal deities. The poojari or temple priest is still lower, for he is openly engaged in worshipping and teaching the worship of impossible idols. The philosophical Brahmans have entirely given up such things, and live upon the produce of lands granted to them in former times. Most of the songs now given have been coolly appropriated by this class and published as "translations from the Sanscrit;"—a fraud as guilty though not as serious as the mutilations about to be noticed.

THE TRUE GOD.

God is the one great *all*. Can such as He,
Eternal Being, see our praise or prayer
In outward acts? If thou wouldst worship Him,
Lift up thy heart—in spirit serve thy God.
Some bow themselves, lie prostrate on the earth,
In meditation spend their days. Some tell
Their beads in prayers, or mantras whisper oft,
Pay dues at sacred shrines. All this is nought.
External objects cannot help. They bring
Great grief to those who trust them. Life is thine
And endless bliss, if thou wilt look within.
God may be seen in spread out space: yet I,
Who looked so long, quite failed to catch the sight,
And darkness held me fast in life-long pain.
But now, by Sivam,* I declare that all
That is is God: yet what I see is not.
It and the thousand evils of the world

* The word *Sivam* is the neuter of Siva, and expresses two things.—First, that the bard is nominally a worshipper of Siva. Every respectable man must call the Deity he serves by one of three names, Vishnu, Siva or Brahma. The question is usually decided by birth. Certain castes are conventionally supposed to worship Vishnu, and certain others Siva. It seldom happens that a man changes his deity-name. Secondly, it proves that while the bard worships Siva, he does so only on the understanding that his deity is not to be considered a *person*. God is an essence or spirit and therefore without sex. The protest against idolatry generally takes this form; as it must be at once understood, even by the most ignorant, that there can be nothing in common between the neuter spirit and the masculine representation which idolatry gives to the personages it delights to honor.

Are not of God nor true. They Maya are.*
Though He doth dwell in everything, the fool
Discerneth not. From him the Godhead hides.
To him who knows, the hidden stands revealed—
The real becomes the seen: but yet not seen,†
For God hath neither form nor earthly frame—
A spirit only. Nor is there any priest
But he that teacheth thus of Deity.
In majesty and bliss, in glory vast,
The great Intelligence pervades and fills

* This verse seems to contain a contradiction. It arises from the form of the last affirmation. When the poet says—"All that is is God: yet what I see is not"—he means that the impression made upon him by the external world is not a true representation of such reality as the external world possesses. The maxim is so condensed that, for a European, it must be somewhat enlarged as follows.—"All that really exists is but a portion of the Godhead. But my senses are so imperfect, and I can so imperfectly understand what my senses exhibit, that the impression my mind at last receives does not at all correspond with the reality of the thing I seem to perceive. By trusting to my senses I am led astray." The ignorant man judges the earth from the evidence of his senses, and never dreams of asking what it really is as intended and brought into existence by God. It—the image of the earth on his retina and still more upon his mind—"is not of God nor true." He knows the world only by his own five senses, which have no more to do with external objects than the painter's brush and oils with the landscape he represents. He thinks he knows what the world *is*, because he is conscious that it has certain effects upon his own nerves—these effects he takes to be the thing itself. He therefore makes a mistake, is led astray by his own ignorance. Before he can have even the slightest knowledge of external things, he must learn that his internal sensations have nothing to do with the reality of the things which they seem to bring to his notice and knowledge.

† Here again is a paradox caused by using the word *seen* in two senses. The same play upon words is in the original. The phrase when enlarged runs thus—"The real becomes perceptible by the mind, but remains imperceptible by the eye."

Each part of all the universe. What then
Is great and what is small? Who is my friend,
And who my foe—if He have thought him good:
If this I love, and that I hate, have I
The right to blame what God hath known it wise
To show? Will then the wise repeat such things?
The wise man sees that living souls surround
His life, and one Intelligence doth rule
In all. He turns with sad and loathing soul
From penance, meditation, outward rites,
And all the cant of sects—from unreal things
That can but bar the road to peace and bliss—
Becomes the loving servant of the truth,
Disciple of a real and faithful priest.

The song—True knowledge—is one of a series known as "Pattanattu's Psalms." The author and a still more eminent poet, Patirakiriyar, lived in the tenth century, about the time of the English king Canute. Both poets had been possessed of great wealth, but a sense of the vanity of worldly things caused them to give up all and live in privation and pain. They were strongly opposed to the then growing influence of idolatry, and poured out bitter but highly poetic satires on the influence of caste and idolatry. Patirakiriyar is the author of some of the "Songs of Sorrow" referred to on page 12. A few stanzas may not be inappropriate in connection with Pattanattu's song. They are taken almost at random from a modern edition, but fairly represent the scope of the book, which is exceedingly popular and often reprinted.

When may I know the hidden things of life
And thus attain perfection? I would show
How false the Vedas are, with error rife:
And burn the Shasters; so the truth might grow.

Oh, when will mankind learn to use aright
The carved stones, the clay baked hard with fire,
The burnished copper shining in the light,
And not to worship them as Gods require?

When shall our race be one great brotherhood
Unbroken by the tyranny of caste,
Which Kapila in early days withstood
And taught that men were one in times now passed?

When may my thoughts be fixed alone on Him
Who is Himself all sweetness, made all things,
Whom all the Vedas sought, though seeing dim,
Who saveth him that to His mercy clings?

When will my God attract to Him my soul
And keep it ever near, beneath His care?
Just as a magnet draws, as to a goal,
Unto itself the weighty iron bar.

When will that God who hath no earthly shape,
Of all the end, and yet who maketh all,
Whose clear pervading eye nought can escape
Accept my service, all my soul enthral?

There is much more to the like purpose, but we must pass on to the song of Pattanattu.

TRUE KNOWLEDGE.

1. My God is not a chiselled stone,
Or lime, so bright and white:
Nor is he cleaned with tamarind,
Like images of bronze.

2. I cannot worship such as these,
But loudly make my boast
That in my heart I place the feet,
The golden feet of God.

3. If He be mine what can I need?
My God is everywhere.
Within, beyond man's highest word,
My God existeth still.

4. In sacred books, in darkest night,
In deepest, bluest sky,
In those who know the truth, and in
The faithful few on earth;—

5. My God is found in all of these,
But can the Deity
Descend to images of stone
Or copper dark and red?

6. Where'er wind blows or compass points,
God's light doth stream and shine,
Yet see yon fool—beneath his arm
He bears the sacred roll.

7. How carefully he folds the page
And draws the closing string!
See how he binds the living book
That not a leaf escape!

8. Ah! Yes; the truth should fill his heart,
But 'tis beneath his arm.
To him who "knows," the sun is high;
To this, 'tis starless night.

9. If still, oh sinful man, with ash
Thou dost besmear thy face,
Or bathest oft, that thus thy soul
May cast away its load.

10. Thou knowest naught of God, nor of
Regeneration's work.
Your mantras, what are they? The Veds
Are burdened with their weight.

11. If knowledge be not thine, thou art
As one in deep mid-stream:
A stream so wide that both the banks
Are hidden from thine eyes.

12. Alas! How long did I adore
The chiselled stone, and serve
An image made of lime or brass
That's cleaned with tamarind.

THE SIN OF IDOLATRY.

1. Men cannot know from whence they came,
Else they would never call the sun
Or moon their God. They would not bow
To idols made of clay, or mud
Baked in the fire. No image made
Of stone or wood, no linga stump,
Built up of earth and made by hand
Could ever seem divine to one
Who knew he came from God.

Some say
That eight plain letters hold all truth,*
And some that it doth dwell in five!
No wonder that such living fools
Exalt Vishnu, and Siva praise.

* It is common in the obscure mysticism to which the more reasonable aspects of Puranism have descended, to count the letters forming the name of the deity that is honored, and say that all wisdom may be found in them. The eight letters here spoken of form the name of Vishnu and the five the name of Siva. A great number of books commence with an invocation in the same style, greatly resembling the illustrated alphabets of which our infants are so fond,—where A stands for apple, B for bear, and so on. All the Hindu "ologies" can thus be brought into the name of the deity. Curious examples of this practice will be seen in the subsequent pages referring to Sivavakyer. There is another and unobjectionable mode of using the first and last letters of the alphabet. Thus, in the Bible, God is said to be Alpha and Omega, the first and the last. Patirakiriyar says—"When will the time come for me to understand the hidden meaning of the letter A, the first of all letters, and know its full meaning." The Cural commences with a similar comparison of Deity with the letter A. Very many of the better poets exhibit the same idea.

2. A hundred thousand living things—
From elephants to tiny ants—
Abound throughout the world. Not one
Of all but has somewhat of God.
The outward sense cannot perceive
This inner sacred habitant.
But turn the vision of thy mind
Upon thine inward self, and then,
As perfume from the blushing flower,
Thou shalt perceive what mortal eye
May never see. Thou then art wise.

3. For those who call a stone their God,
Or dream that Kasi or Sathu*
Can cleanse them from their sin,—for those
Who take a part in heathen rites,
Who murder, steal, or throw the dice,
Speak falsely for their gain or friend,
The seven dark hells do gape. They wait
Until the time of fate be come
And sinners meet the doom they earn.†
When time shall turn again, and life
Shall come to some, these men shall pine
In stones for seven painful births.

* Kasi is the native name for Benares. Sathu is the sacred island of Ramĕswaram, in the strait that separates India from Ceylon. The south of India is full of sacred places to which pilgrims come each year by thousands. Some of the most eminent are Mylapore, Tripathy, Trivellore, Seringham, Tanjore and Conjeveram. The spread of education is gradually but surely killing the system. The number of pilgrims diminishes every year.

† See note on next page. It is not often that the retributive character of hell is so clearly stated. The profitable sacerdotal doctrine that sin is punished by new births, and that these may be prevented by due offerings and repeated ceremonies, has gradually supplanted the earlier truth.

4. How mad are ye who offer praise
To carven stones! As if such things
Could fitly image God most High!
Can He be but a dirty stone?
And can such worship reach His ear?
Be faithful to the glorious priest
Who teaches truth. Receive from him
The heavenly light that shall make clear
What body is and what is soul.
Let all thy mind be overwhelmed
With that great blaze of light which beams,
From what is typified by "Om."*

5. Who teach that copper, stones, or wood
Are Gods, and also those who follow them,
Shall never reach the blessed home,
But perish in the seven dark hells.†

* *Om*, or more properly *Aum*, is a mystic word of which no one knows the real meaning. It is used for a hundred different things; as each writer has a different idea of a something that pervades the world and yet is not God. It is supposed to typify a mysterious excellence which is of God and yet is not God. It enshrines the essence of the Trimurtti or Hindu Trinity and is something beyond Vishnu or Siva, yet not greater than they. It is the essence of the Vedas. It is infinite wisdom and mysticism. It is the highest summit of every thing that man should aspire to, yet is utterly beyond even the greatest of Rishis, and they can be more than Gods.

† The Hindu theory of transmigration does not prevent their having hells. There is, almost invariably, an immense period of time between death and the next birth, and through that period the soul suffers or enjoys accordingly to its merits. There is a chapter in the Mahabharatá of singular interest, seeing that it anticipates Dante's Inferno. As with Dante, hell is divided into circles of particular punishments, and the leading sins on earth have each their peculiar retribution. The parallel is often very close, and the whole chapter is well worthy of translation.

THE UNITY OF GOD.

1. Into the bosom of the one great sea
Flow streams that come from hills on every side.
Their names are various as their springs.
And thus in every land do men bow down
To one great God, though known by many names.
This mighty Being we would worship now.

2. What though the six religions* loudly shout
That each alone is true, all else are false?
Yet when in each the wise man worships God,
The great almighty *One* receives the prayer.

3. Oh Lord, when may I hope
To find the clue that leads
From out the labyrinth
Of brawling erring sects?

4. Six blind men once described an elephant
That stood before them all. One felt the back.
The second noticed pendent ears. The third
Could only find the tail. The beauteous tusks
Absorbed the admiration of the fourth.
While of the other two, one grasped the trunk.
The last sought for small things and found
Four thick and clumsy feet. From what each learned,
He drew the beast. Six monsters stood revealed.
Just so the six religions learned of God,
And tell their wondrous tales. Our God is one.

* All these songs were written before the advent of Europeans, and the six religions do not include Christianity. Very different accounts of them are given, but they may be supposed to be Buddhists, Jains, Vedantists, Vaishnavas, Shivas, and Lingayets.

5. Men talk of penance, fastings, sacred streams—
Make pilgrimage to temples, offer gifts;
Performing to the letter all the rules
Of senseless complicated ritual.
Yet are they doomed to sorrow's deepest pain.
Oh, fling such things away and fix thy heart
On rest and peace to come. Seek that alone.

6. To them that fully know the heavenly truth,
There is no good or ill; nor anything
To be desired, unclean or purely clean.
To them there is no good can come from fast
Or penance pains. To them the earth has naught
For hope or fear, in thought or word or deed.*

7. They hear the four great Vedas shout aloud
That he who has true wisdom in his heart
Can have no thought for fleeting worldly things.
Where God is seen, there can be naught but God.
His heart can have no place for fear or shame,
For caste, uncleanness, hate or wandering thought.
Impure and pure are all alike to him.

* This verse is one of those that appear to countenance the grosser impurities of life. If nothing be unclean or bad, if there be no fear of evil consequences for immoral actions, why may not we live only for the flesh? This is the very argument employed by Sakti worshippers, by the Maharajahs of Bombay and others who teach similar doctrines. Yet it is quite clear that the verse cannot lead to this inference. It is only " to them who fully know the heavenly truth," that nothing is unclean or bad. But the very fact assumes that they have overcome their senses—they have no desire—they think only on God—they have left the world. As another song asserts, youth or beauty have no charm for them. They cannot even be tempted to immorality, for its essence is fleshly pleasure, and this they have eschewed. Evil results follow only when those who do not "know" take upon themselves the privileges of those who do. To them things may be and are both unclean and utterly bad.

The "Brotherhood of Man" is especially worthy of notice. Its morality is so high and its imagery so vivid that I have translated it as literally as possible without rhymes. In its present form it professes to have been rendered from a Sanscrit original, but this is merely a literary fraud, perpetrated probably by the printer, in order to make the publication acceptable to his Brahman customers. It is another incidental link in the chain of facts showing how diligently the literary caste have taught that nothing good can come from any other source. It is in reality the work of Kapila, who is said to have been the brother of Tiruvalluva. That it is very ancient is shown by a verse of Patirakiriyar, quoted on a previous page, which, though itself written in the tenth century, speaks of Kapila, referring probably to this very song, as having so "taught in the beginning." That is, Kapila was then an ancient writer. It helps to establish what has been assumed in the pages concerning Tiruvalluva, that he dates from about the third century. The song was probably a part of Kapila's Agaval. If so, it has been separated from the context and somewhat modified by popular use, since the Agaval, as we have it, does not contain the precise passage, although there is much of the same tenor. Seldom has the argument for the essential unity of mankind been more pithily expressed, and it says much for the inner heart of the nation that the song should have survived and remain so popular.

THE BROTHERHOOD OF MAN.

BY KAPILA.

1. Oh Brahmans, list to me
And answer if you can.
When ye at funeral rites
Do represent the dead,
Receiving in your hands
The precious things and food
His sons so freely give ;—

2. When solemn rites are made
With every offering ;—
Have you or yours e'er seen
The spirit hands outstretched
Because they need the food ?
Or have you seen them close
When hunger is assuaged ?

3. Do rain and wind avoid
Some men among the rest
Because their caste is low ?
When such men tread the earth
Hast seen it quake with rage ?
Or does the brilliant sun
Refuse to them its rays ?

4. Oh Brahmans, has our God
E'er bid the teeming fields
Bring forth the fruit and flowers
For men of caste alone ?
Or made the forest green
To gratify the eyes
Of none but Pariahs ?

5. Such wealth as men may have,
Such biting poverty,
Aye, even death itself,
Are but the common lot
Of all that dwell on earth,—
The logical results
Of deeds of good or bad.*

6. Our deeds may never die,
And even now we rue
What, in our former births,
We did or left undone.
To this alone we owe
That we have bliss or pain,
Have hope or deep despair.

7. Oh Brahmans, list to me!
In all this blessed land
There is but one great caste,
One tribe and brotherhood.
One God doth dwell above,
And he hath made us one
In birth and frame and tongue.

8. If therefore, O ye fools,
Ye would observe and do
The precepts of your sires,
Give alms to all who need,
And, as for life, avoid
All that is mean, or smacks
Of lies and knavery.

* This and the next verse are the key to much of the Dravidian argument explaining the inequalities of this life, and the doctrine of transmigration. God is not to be blamed if we are poor or unhappy—we suffer what we have ourselves created.

9. Virtue alone is strong,
And fears no present pain.
Its life may never end,
Nor can its joys abate;
For virtue's self is peace.
Learn virtue then, my friend,
And give thy life to it.

TRUE WORSHIP.

BY SIVAVAKYER.

1. When once I knew the Lord
What were to me the host
Of pagan deities?
Some fixed in temple shrines,
Or carried in the crowd;
Some made of unbaked clay,
And some burnt hard with fire?
With all the lying tales
That fill the sacred books
They've vanished from my mind.

2. Of two stones on the hill,
The first you take and carve—
Into an idol make.
You rub with sandal ash,
Adorn with brilliant flowers,
And worship it as God.
The next serves for a road—
You tread it underfoot.
In neither can our God
Take pleasure or delight.

3. How many flowers I gave
   At famous temple shrines!
How many mantras said!
   Oft washed the idol's head!
And still with weary feet
   Encircled Siva's shrines!
But now at last I know
   Where dwells the king of Gods,
And never will salute
   A temple made with hands.

4. But yet I have a shrine—
   The mind within my breast.
A linga* too is there—
   The soul that came from God.
I offer ash and flowers—
   The praises of my heart.
And all the God-made world,
   Is frankincense and myrrh.
And thus, where'er I go,
   I ever worship God.

5. Ye knaves and fools, who boast
   How well and much you write!
No ass can bray so loud
   As ye proclaim your skill.

* The linga, the Grecian phallus, is the emblem of creation and the special symbol of all who worship Siva. It is a curious instance of the mode in which Brahmanism has mutilated the religious thought it found in existence, that Siva, in the Hindu triad, is always the destroyer. The worshippers of Siva never countenanced this. With them Siva is purely the Creator, the maker and upholder of all that is. The Brahmanic triad is but the clumsy effort of the sacerdotal caste to comprehend the other religions it found in India with its own,—an ill-assorted group of erroneously described figures, varnished with legend made for the purpose of hiding imperfections as they came to light.

And yet your souls lie prone
In flesh that creeps with worms.
Oh, will you never learn
How petty such things are?
Strive with your might to gain
The one eternal truth.

6. E'en if you read the Veds,
The Sama and the Rik;
And know the Shasters' six;
You still may never know
The great divine Sivam.
Yet if you will but turn
From flesh and its desires,
Suppressing lust and shame,
Your eyes and heart may see
The Being that is God.

7. You utter lies in hosts
While books are in your hands.
Yea, pour them out afresh
As many as you wish!
But know that soon will come
Your dreaded final day
When God will judge aright.
All they that know the Lord,
The great unknown first cause,
Are blest with wisdom high.

The corrupting efforts of the Brahmans, as exercised on old Dravidian literature, have so often been referred to that the reader may think the feeling exaggerated. On the other hand all will feel the exceeding beauty of the song just rendered, and will be inclined to speak with severity of those who would mutilate it. It will not therefore, be deemed too great a digression to give the opening chapter of the works of Sivavakyer, as expurgated and improved by the sacerdotal class. It cannot be promised that any one will understand it. I went over it carefully with a learned Brahman and failed to extract any connected sense from it, nor was my guide more successful. When pressed for an abstract of its meaning he replied—"That is the way we talk when we mean to say that Siva is the greatest God."

1. Many bodies come from A;
   They stand so firm with O.
   Through M the world was dark,
   But S sets all things free.

The first three letters make the mystic word AOM or AUM, which has already been referred to. The letter S is the initial of Siva, and is supposed to state that even AUM itself is of no force unless Siva guides it.

2. Essential Nama-sivayum,
   He is both beginning and end.
   He is twelve crores, a countless host,
   He is all mantras, the four Vedas,
   The six Shastras, all the puranas.
   Vishnu and Brahma seek after him.
   He is almighty God, God, God.

Nama-sivayum is the "name of Siva." A crore is ten millions. The mantras are mystic sentences supposed to have power over the Gods.

3. Nama-sivayum has five letters,
These are all things that remain on earth.
Nama-sivayum has five letters,
But he has one more.
Nama-sivayum is the five elements,
The other one stands for king.
Oh Nama-sivayum, teach me the truth.

4. *Na* means two legs, *Ma* is the stomach,
Si is two arms, *Va* is the mouth.
Ya is two eyes, and why they both were made.
So out of five letters we see Sivayum,
Agreeable, beautiful, standing.

5. Heaven can be gained in Siva's five letters,
Siva's five letters will conquer Heaven.
True wisdom is known from Siva's five letters,
Deeply consider the five letters of Siva.

A few verses quoted at random will still better explain how the book has been metamorphosed. It seems to have been born again in some lower world, and to teach an altogether new doctrine. We commence with one that directly contradicts the whole tenor of Sivavakyer's teaching,

Five and three are eight—
Eight original mantras.
If you keep them in mind,
Tell them hundreds of times,
Then your sins fly away
Like to cotton in wind;
Though a billion they are.
So I learn from the Veds.

There is a wandering vital air,
It flows through all the living frame.
If with your mind you seize this breath
And lift it to your head, its force
Will make the old man young again.
New strength will come to weakened limbs.
By Siva and his lovely wife I swear
That every word I say is true.

The Vedas four and those who study them,—
The wisdom that thus comes to those who read,—
The poison-drunken Rudra,—Brahma too,—
And Vishnu,—All these deeply meditate
On one great object—Nama-sivayum.

But this will surely be enough to show how careful has been the corruption, how skilful the mutilation that has in time landed Sivavakyer in such a plight. It has been done gradually, here a little and there a little, line upon line, so that the masses might not know how their food was being stolen from them.

The peculiar audacity of the mutilation does not appear so strongly until we remember that, in the original, the words Siva and Vishnu do not once appear except for censure. In its new form, almost every verse of the poem contains the name of Siva, and the opening chapter can speak of nothing else. The subject cannot be better closed than with the following extract from Taylor's Oriental Manuscripts (Vol. 3, page 26.) The work of Sivavakyer "is a didactic moral poem, characterized chiefly by its monotheistical purport. It is very severe on idol-worship and on various abuses connected with the common *Brahmanical* system; maintaining the necessity of rejecting the names of Siva and Vishnu, and worshipping one only God. Hence it has always been made great use of by Native Christians, in disputing with Hindu natives. I was told, some years ago, that the *ascetics* (or *Pandarams*) of the Saiva class seek after copies of this poem with avidity, and uniformly destroy every copy they find. It is, by consequence, rather scarce and chiefly preserved by the Native Christians......I have had one good copy carefully restored......The restoration was of the greater consequence, because of a proceeding of the *Dherma Sabha* at Madras. As the book could not be destroyed, they caused to be printed an interpolated and greatly corrupted version, as the genuine work of the author, but maintaining just the reverse of his real opinions."

This is but one specimen of a process that has been going on for centuries, deliberately aiming at the destruction of all early Dravidian literature. The process has gone so far that the greater part of Sivavakyer cannot now be called folk-literature so much as relics of ancient folk-literature. Hence I have given but one song, which has been separated from his other works by the people and kept floating among them. This is therefore truly a folk-song. Having said so much about him, however, the student will be glad to compare genuine stanzas of the chief work of Sivavakyer with the corrupted passages before quoted. The following are a few pearls among the many strung together to form the poem:

Our God an ocean is, infinity;
No eye can see the end. He has no bound.
He who would see and know Him must repress
The waves of his own heart, must be at peace.
His sole desire is God. His every sense
Must turn to that great One and clasp but Him.

There is no real but He,—the One that fills
All space. He dwelleth everywhere. The sun
That sends its light through all the lower world
Pervades much less than He. Yet men deny
And will not know their God. They love to lie
In mire of sin. But I have learned of Him,
And find no single thing in all the world
To show how great His glory. Words must fail
To tell the joy, the bliss, I have in Him:
Yet when I try no man believes my speech.

That highest One is not a beauteous rose,
Nor doth He hide Him in the sweet perfume.
What men ascribe to Him, that is He not.
He is not great, much less can He be small.
The voice that speaks is not the Lord, nor can
He be shut in or out. He hath no shape,
Nor dwelleth only in some single thing.
This Infinite surpasseth all our thoughts.

There is but One in all the world, none else.
That one is God, the Lord of all that is,
He never had beginning, never hath an end.

Oh God! I once knew nought of what Thou art,
And wandered far astray. But when Thy light
Pierced through my dark, I woke to know my God.
Oh Lord! I long for Thee alone. I long
For none but Thee to dwell within my soul.

When Thou didst make me, Thou didst know my all.
But I knew not of Thee. 'Twas not till light
From Thee gave me to understand of Thee
That I could know. But now where'er I sit,
Or walk, or stand, Thou art for ever near.
Can I forget Thee? Thou art mine; and I
Am only Thine. E'en with these eyes I see,
And with my heart perceive, that Thou art come
To me as lightning from the lowering sky.

If thy poor heart but choose the better part,
And in this path doth worship only God,
His heart will stoop to thine, will take thy heart
And make it His. One heart shall serve for both.

When thy poor mind has always God within,
The highest One will surely dwell with thee:
Will rob thee of thy sins. As with his tool
The artisan will shave or cut clean off
Each roughness from the wood, so He will make
Thee free from sin and altogether pure.

To lay her eggs the turtle swimmeth far
To reach the sandy shore. She buries them
And swimmeth back again. Yet doth her mind
Adhere to them. When young ones break their shell
They feel the tie. It draws them as a rope
Along their mother's path.* At last they meet.
Just so hath God placed us. We wander here
While He is far above. Yet in His mind
We ever stay. The tie doth reach to earth
From highest heaven. If we but follow it,
We cannot fail to reach and live with Him.

Some think to find their God upon the hills,
And climb with weary feet. So some declare
He is beyond the sea. They sail afar
To find Him out. Oh ignorant and fools!
'Tis pride that prompts your work. His sacred feet
Are in your heart. If there you seek, your soul
Will find the Being that alone is real.

Not for a single moment has my God
Forgotten helpless me. Oh only God!
My king and king of kings! I could not live
One moment without Thee. One mercy more
Bestow—that praise may dwell upon my tongue.

* The verse refers to a popular idea that, when the young turtle is able to trust himself to the sea, he swims straight towards his parent. Though the sea is boundless and pathless he can find his way, for the mother's love draws him unconsciously towards her. The figure as applied to the mode in which God acts upon the souls of men is very beautiful.

Is it any wonder that old Ziegenbalg, the pioneer of Protestant Missions in India, should exclaim—"From all this it is sufficiently evident what these heathens believe of God, the Supreme Being, and how much further they have come in his knowledge by the light of nature, than the heathens of Rome. But the light of nature has been quite obscured by their ancient (Sanskrit) poets and Brahmans, who have written many fabulous stories, and introduced a confused idol-worship, out of which they cannot easily extricate themselves, though they feel much opposition to it in their consciences, and can speak very reasonably of the Supreme Being."

We turn from these highly wrought protests against idolatry to an altogether different class of songs—the labor strains of the working people. They were all taken down on the spot as they were sung by a gang of coolies engaged in arduous manual labor. The custom follows that of the English sailor—one member of the gang gives the strain, the rest join in the chorus. It generally happens on board-ship, however, that the singer is the same throughout, and is exempted from great muscular exertion as a recompense for the stimulant his song gives to the others. In coolie gangs they usually take turns with the strain, each man giving a complete song. Of course it often happens that one or more of the men cannot sing and they never rise higher than the chorus, but they are exceptions to the rule. Some of the songs are in long lines slowly repeated; these are employed where the work requires great effort exerted at comparatively long intervals. Others, and notably the last, are intended to accompany rapid but less strenuous effort.

The palankeen bearers are great singers, very fond of having a sharp revenge on stingy employers by inventing impromptu verses reflecting on their physical and moral characteristics and those of their female relatives. So few Europeans understand them that they offend almost with impunity. I remember a stout gentleman who had hired bearers to carry him up the ghaut, but who was either so impecunious or illiberal as not to offer a handsome present in consideration of his unusual weight. Unfortunately he knew low Tamil well. Hardly were they well on the ghaut before his torment commenced. Mile after mile produced a portrait of him by some new hand. It was undignified to protest. It was beyond human nature to be patient. He fumed with rage. He ordered them to be quiet—he wished to sleep. They obeyed for a while, and then again broke forth the monotonous wail against the untoward fate that compelled them to carry a mountain up a mountain. They gained their end, though not in the way they wanted. The traveller would not give, and could not put up with their comments. When still a mile or more from the top, he dismissed the bearers, and resolved to trust to his own powers of climbing. Hours afterwards, a weary but corpulent way-farer crawled into Coonoor—a sorrowful victim of Dravidian impromptus.

The labor songs are the utterance of an illiterate

class. They are almost unintelligible to a respectable caste-man. The language holds about the same relation to literary Tamil as the Keighley dialect to the English of Macaulay. It will be seen they are not without humour; that about wives is exceedingly rich. How the Bayadere's song sprang up among coolies it is not easy to see, unless it be due to the common re-active feeling which makes the worker dream of the happiness of the idle, and the hungry delight in visions of luxurious meals. It must be remembered that the Bayadere or dancing-girl is not contemned like an English prostitute. Popular respect, and the absence of all sense of moral guilt on their own part, have ensured that they should respect themselves. There is no class of native society less frequently before the criminal courts than the dancing-girl, that is, the professional prostitute. There are hundreds of abandoned women, of whom this cannot be said, but they belong to an entirely different class. The song, therefore, really amounts to no more than such an envious effusion as might spring to the lips of some poor London laborer when witnessing or dreaming of the life of the "gilded youth" of Belgravia or Mayfair.

The first is a joyous offering to Pillaiyar, commonly known as the Belly God. His respectable name is Ganesa. He is universally venerated as the God of good luck, the remover of difficulties. The poorer classes are especially fond of him—their whole life is one series of difficulties, and who then so welcome as Pillaiyar. He is represented with an elephant's head and an enormous stomach, so that his name is very appropriate. There is a close connection between Ganesa and Saraswati the goddess of learning, inasmuch as Ganesa will only remove such obstacles as cannot, by the aid of knowledge, be surmounted. The ordinary mythology makes them brother and sister.

LABOUR SONGS.

1. Pillaiyar brings good luck to you,
   And Saraswati wit.
   Ho! Ho! work hard!

   The God was born before Kudu.*
   O clear our way some whit!
   Ho! Ho! work hard!

2. Ere Aluvar thou wast, I ween.
   Pillaiyar, clear our way!
   Ho! Ho! work hard!

   Beneath the banyan and the neem
   To Pillaiyar I'll pray.
   Ho! Ho! work hard!

* Proper names are so altered in the coolie patois, that it is doubtful what Kudu and Aluvar in the next verse refer to. The latter may be a corrupt form of the word *alvar* and refer to one of the twelve rishis of Southern India. It may, however, be that both words describe more homely things, and that *kudu* is but another form of *kudi*, a house; and *aluvar* another form of *aluval*, business, labor. In that case the words would mean that Pillaiyar was anterior to the present state of things, before there was work to be done or houses to be built.

3. Oh, young Pillaiyar's golden feet
I never will forget.
Ho! Ho! work hard!
Oh kind Pillaiyar, when we meet
How shall I pay my debt?
Ho! Ho! work hard!

4. I'll take green gram and mix it well
With ten full pounds of rice,—
Ho! Ho! work hard!
And add oil seeds—how rich they smell—
They make the rice so nice.
Ho! Ho! work hard!

5. Take then a heap of sugar-cane,—
'Twould serve to drive the ewes;—*
Ho! Ho! work hard!
Aye, e'en picotta-work would gain
By using such bamboos.
Ho! Ho! work hard!

* This and the next verse mean that the sugar-cane stick he will offer shall be of the finest. It shall be strong enough to drive sheep and cattle with. It shall be long and thick enough to serve as the rod for a picotta, a machine for raising water from deep wells by hanging a bucket at the end of a long pole and then attaching the other end of the pole to one arm of an elevated horizontal lever. The weight of a man on the other end of the lever raises the pole and with it the water. This apparatus is found to be the most efficient means of raising water in a land where coal is costly. It is another instance of the mode in which Hindoos have very frequently hit upon the very best means of employing natural forces for human purposes. No European engineer would have dreamt of such a contrivance—so simple and so inelegant—yet none can supersede it. The Railway companies have tried every possible device and the best of English machinery, but have been driven back on the picotta.

6. Then pluck some jack that hangs so great
   Just at the tree's gnarled root.*
      Ho! Ho! work hard!
   And from the guava tree its weight
   Of sweet and luscious fruit.
      Ho! Ho! work hard!

7. In bringing these I bear in mind
   To gather leaves of green.
      Ho! Ho! work hard!
   Ascending northern slopes, I find
   The plantain's verdant sheen.
      Ho! Ho! work hard!

8. Upon the southern side there grow
   The taper leaves of teak.
      Ho! Ho! work hard!
   The flower that out of reach doth blow
   I with a ladder seek.
      Ho! Ho! work hard!

9. Then with a crook and knife are shorn
   The buds both rich and rare.
      Ho! Ho! work hard!
   And soon the opening flowers adorn
   Some lock of jet black hair.
      Ho! Ho! work hard!

* The gigantic fruit of the Jack-tree does not hang from the smaller twigs as with most other fruit trees. The fruit is so large and heavy that anything less than a thick bough would be broken by its weight. So it hangs from the trunk and strongest branches. The largest specimens will often be found within a few feet of the ground.

BAYADERE'S SONG.

WITH MORAL.

1. From the banks of the Ganges the water they brought
   In a vessel of brass.
   Heave O! Heave O!
   I have washéd my feet as a dancing girl ought,
   And have wiped them with silk.
   Heave O! Heave O!

2. Let us go then, oh girls, before Madavan's* shrine:
   Let us worship him now.
   Heave O! Heave O!
   If we offer our flowers to the image divine,
   We may hope for new joys.
   Heave O! Heave O!

3. What delight can exceed those of love and desire?
   And all these are for us!
   Heave O! Heave O!
   Oh my girls, like the pea-hen in mien and attire,
   I was born for the dance.
   Heave O! Heave O!

4. What a joy to be born as a girl for the dance!
   And what more can I want?
   Heave O! Heave O!
   What a pleasure to feel I can do with a glance
   More than kings on their throne!
   Heave O! Heave O!

* Madavan is abbreviated and corrupted from Mahadevan or the great God—a title usually applied to Siva.

Moral (by an ill-tempered man)

5. I would rather remain but a lump of vile clay
Than be only a girl.
Heave O! Heave O!
For a potter can make it a pot any day,
And 'tis therefore of use.
Heave O! Heave O!

The song entitled "Mother" probably combines the divine with the human, the goddess with the nurse. The lower classes in the Tamil country worship very largely a set of deities called Gramadēvatas or village deities. These with two exceptions, Ayenar and Virabhadra, are all females and take the title *amma* or mother. The chief of them are Ellamma, Agathamma, Mariamma, Ankalamma and Bhadrakali, also called mātā or mother. The little pagodas belonging to these deities are found almost everywhere. The traveller in the interior will often have noticed near such "Swamy-houses" a grotesque collection of hollow figures of horses, elephants, demons, &c., made of burnt clay and then glaringly colored. These images are offerings made by grateful worshippers who suppose themselves to have been preserved from danger or death by the deity. One of the finest collections I have ever seen is near the railway station at Caroor in Tanjore. Along the coast, north of Madras, are regular hills composed entirely of the debris of such images, proving how great the manufacture must have been in former times. Thinly scattered fishermen's huts are the only signs of habitation now. The reader will be able to judge as to which of the verses are intended to applied to the earthly mother. It is probable that every one has either a direct or indirect reference to the deity.

MOTHER.

1. We have bowed three times at your feet;
   We have bowed our head.
   Yo Ho! Yo Ho!
   Oh our mother, our thanks we repeat;
   And we wait in dread.
   Yo Ho! Yo Ho!

2. We were born of thee, and our hope
   Is in none but thee.
   Yo Ho! Yo Ho!
   Give us food and a sword; else we mope,
   And from foes we flee.
   Yo Ho! Yo Ho!

3. Oh! How loud we shout, for we yearn
   Thy bright face to see!
   Yo Ho! Yo Ho!
   We have sought thee long, and we burn
   For thy love so free.
   Yo Ho! Yo Ho!

4. Like a pearl, mamma, is thy mouth,
May it speak again!
Yo Ho! Yo Ho!
In my need, distress and in drouth,
I have begged in vain.
Yo Ho! Yo Ho!

5. And for whom, I ask, is the grace
That by right is mine?
Yo Ho! Yo Ho!
Sons-in-law, their kin, or their race,
Who are nought of thine?
Yo Ho! Yo Ho!

6. Oh return, mamma, to your son!
I will then be still.
Yo Ho! Yo Ho!
Thou hast had five sons, and hast known
Of the pangs they feel.
Yo Ho! Yo Ho!

7. Thou hast known our hearts and the pain.
That doth break them now.
Yo Ho! Yo Ho!
Thou canst not thy love so refrain
As to scorn our vow.
Yo Ho! Yo Ho!

8. As for her, my love, who has none
Of her own to guard,—
Yo Ho! Yo Ho!
How can she share the pain of a son,
Or his woes regard?
Yo Ho! Yo Ho!

9. In your pain and love I was born,
   And you gave my name.
      Yo Ho! Yo Ho!
 All the day, at night, and at morn,
   You have fed my flame.
      Yo Ho! Yo Ho!

10. As a field of milk you were then,
   And in it I fed.
      Yo Ho! Yo Ho!
 As a pot of ghee to poor men,
   You were thus my bread.
      Yo Ho! Yo Ho!

11. And yet now with pain I am racked,
   And my heart is fire.
      Yo Ho! Yo Ho!
 And my side, how long has it ached!
   And the pangs are dire.
      Yo Ho! Yo Ho!

12. How my breast, mamma, doth up-heave!
   Let it plead for me!
      Yo Ho! Yo Ho!
 Is it fate, mamma, that I grieve,
   Or my need of thee?
      Yo Ho! Yo Ho!

The following needs no introduction. It will be immediately recognized as no mean member of the great array of poetical attacks upon man's "better half."

THE WIFE.

To every man is tied a wife,
She clings to him as long as life.
Yo Ho! Heave O!

Of all our wealth she takes two-thirds,
Yet thinks we pick up more like birds.
Yo Ho! Heave O!

If any day we give her none,
You'd think her wrath would ne'er be done.
Yo Ho! Heave O!

While still 'tis dark she turns us out,
But sleeps for two hours more, no doubt!
Yo Ho! Heave O!

We toil all day with spade or bar;
To bring our dinner 'tis too far.
Yo Ho! Heave O!

Oh! How we strain and heave and sweat;
While she buys cloths and runs in debt!
Yo Ho! Heave O!

No moment may we stay to rest;
She works an hour a day at best.
Yo Ho! Heave O!

We are too busy e'en to eat;
She scarcely ever leaves her seat.
Yo Ho! Heave O!

What comes of all the wage we earn?
Ah! that from her no man can learn.
Yo Ho! Heave O!

Our breasts are bruised by rope and pole;
That ne'er prevents her daily stroll.
Yo Ho! Heave O!

Our pain is more than we can bear;
She combs and oils her jet-black hair.
Yo Ho! Heave O!

Sometimes we faint through heat and toil;
To sweep the house her cloth would soil!
Yo Ho! Heave O!

'Tis well if we may earn some pice;
At home her mouth is filled with rice.
Yo Ho! Heave O!

We rest,—the master stops our pay,—
She scolds and bawls till morn is grey.
Yo Ho! Heave O!

How strange and odd a world is this,
To us the work, to them the bliss!
Yo Ho! Heave O!

The following song is interesting as being the only Christian one in the series. Yet it is truly a folk-song. The early Roman Catholic missionaries were very successful among the fishermen and coolies who made the ancient city of St. Thomé their head-quarters. With the peace and physical prosperity introduced by the English, these classes have become very numerous and may be counted in the city of Madras by thousands. Madras has absorbed St. Thomé much as London has absorbed Westminster, and the fisher castes have spread southward, along the coast, for many miles. One of the wealthiest religious corporations in India is the Roman Catholic church of Royapuram, whose large accumulated funds have come entirely from the thousands of poor fishermen who look upon it as their cathedral. The requirements of a large city have withdrawn many fisher families from the sea to utilize them as common day-laborers or coolies, as they are commonly called, from a word meaning daily wages. A large number of pariahs, a still lower class, also became disciples of the self-denying Catholic missionaries, and help to swell the proportion of converts among the laboring class.

The Catholic missionaries, especially the Portuguese, have always shown a strong desire to assimilate Christian ritual and social practice as much as possible with those of the orthodox Hindus. Hence an ordinary observer would not be able to notice any difference between the Christian festival and procession of St. Joseph and the Hindu festival and procession of

Krishna or Pillaiyarswami. This principle led the more capable priests to compose songs and poems, in imitation of those so popular among the worshippers of Vishnu and Shiva. Beschi began the series with lyrics in the high dialect, for the use of the better castes. Others went lower in the scale, and now there is a constant stream of vernacular Christian poesy intended for the masses. Beschi's *Tembavani*, or paraphrase of Scripture, is one of the very finest Tamil poems and is constantly quoted by the pundits as representing the most classical form of high Tamil. It takes an almost equal place beside the Cural for beauty of language, although the text is but a greatly corrupted transcript of the Bible. Other less known poems by Beschi are the *Calivenba, Veda Vilaccum,* and *Gnana Unerttal.* Robert de Nobili had set an example many years before in poems which were then highly esteemed. Beschi's superior talent has, however, driven his precursor out of the field.

The song now to be quoted was sung by a mixed company of coolies, of whom not more than one-third were Christians. It appeared well known to them all, and had doubtless been learnt by constant repetition, as a matter of course, without any thought whether it was Christian or Heathen. Its short lines adapt it for its purpose—to sing when the work required frequent effort at short intervals. After every line came the chorus, "Yellè," a corrupt patois for a word meaning—work hard or well.

CHRISTIAN LABOUR SONG.

1. When time began
Chorus—Yo Ho! Heave Ho!
The mighty Lord
Yo Ho! Heave Ho!
Created man
Yo Ho! Heave Ho!
With but one word.
Yo Ho! Heave Ho!

2. All things depend
Yo Ho! Heave Ho!
On other things,
Yo Ho! Heave Ho!
But from our Friend
Yo Ho! Heave Ho!
They have their springs.
Yo Ho! Heave Ho!

3. Our God and Lord
Yo Ho! Heave Ho!
On earth was born;
Yo Ho! Heave Ho!
By us adored,
Yo Ho! Heave Ho!
In servant's form.
Yo Ho! Heave Ho!

4. Justice and truth
Yo Ho! Heave Ho!
He brought with Him,
Yo Ho! Heave Ho!
His heart was ruth,
Yo Ho! Heave Ho!
His eye not dim.
Yo Ho! Heave Ho!

5. He came to save
Yo Ho! Heave Ho!
All men from sin;
Yo Ho! Heave Ho!
His life He gave
Yo Ho! Heave Ho!
Our life to win.
Yo Ho! Heave Ho!

6. Men broke the law
Yo Ho! Heave Ho!
Our God had made,
Yo Ho! Heave Ho!
Nor stood in awe
Yo Ho! Heave Ho!
Of what He bade.
Yo Ho! Heave Ho!

7. Thus labor came
Yo Ho! Heave Ho!
On all our race;
Yo Ho! Heave Ho!
On man the blame,
Yo Ho! Heave Ho!
From God the grace.
Yo Ho! Heave Ho!

8. The fruit they ate
Yo Ho! Heave Ho!
Of Eden's tree,
Yo Ho! Heave Ho!
A sin so great
Yo Ho! Heave Ho!
Brought all our dree.
Yo Ho! Heave Ho!

9 Since we must work
Yo Ho! Heave Ho!
And feel the curse,
Yo Ho! Heave Ho!
Let us not shirk
Yo Ho! Heave Ho!
Our fate adverse.
Yo Ho! Heave Ho!

10. Time glides away,
Yo Ho! Heave Ho!
Our babes will cry.
Yo Ho! Heave Ho!
How long we stay;
Yo Ho! Heave Ho!
Night cometh nigh.
Yo Ho! Heave Ho!

11. Then let us strive
Yo Ho! Heave Ho!
Till work is done,
Yo Ho! Heave Ho!
Keep heart alive
Yo Ho! Heave Ho!
Till rest is won.
Yo Ho! Heave Ho!

12. Our work is great,
Yo Ho! Heave Ho!
Much yet to do.
Yo Ho! Heave Ho
Time will not wait,
Yo Ho! Heave Ho!
Howe'er we woo.
Yo Ho! Heave Ho!

13. But why so strive?
Yo Ho! Heave Ho!
Our daily pay
Yo Ho! Heave Ho!
Will just contrive
Yo Ho! Heave Ho!
To pay our way.
Yo Ho! Heave Ho!

The last verse sounds like an addition by some workman not at one with the song. He wants to know why they should make haste. They are daily laborers; their pay is enough to keep them alive; if they finish the work to-day, they will want work to-morrow. Why then should they be so anxious to take delight in their curse? That such improvised additions are common, we may be quite sure. The Bayadere's Song has just such another cynical turn tacked on at the end. But there is actual witness to this mode, not of robbery but of addition. As this very song was being taken down, the leader of the singing thought opportunity and his talent combined might cause a good chance of substantial benefit coming out of the occasion. So without a moment's hesitation, and making no sensible breach in the narration, he tacked on the following three verses. The verse just referred to cannot have been invented at the same time, for it distinctly states that their wage is sufficient, while these loudly proclaim how bare a pittance it is.

1. Our pay is small.
Yo Ho! Heave Ho!
Oh kind good Sir!
Yo Ho! Heave Ho!
We one and all
Yo Ho! Heave Ho!
Ask you for more.
Yo Ho! Heave Ho!

2. This kindly man
Yo Ho! Heave Ho!
If we but pray,
Yo Ho! Heave Ho!
He'll find a plan
Yo Ho! Heave Ho!
To give more pay.
Yo Ho! Heave Ho!

3. His Highness then
Yo Ho! Heave Ho!
Will hear our prayer,
Yo Ho! Heave Ho!
And give us men
Yo Ho! Heave Ho!
Good gifts to share.
Yo Ho! Heave Ho!

As these verses were trolled out, the whole company gave the choruses as smartly as if they knew them by heart, and had heard them every day of their lives. It must be confessed, though, that the improvisatore was not equal to the maker of the song itself.

It will seem strange to a western reader that the Cural of Tiruvalluva should be the most venerated and popular book south of the Godavery. To those who know the Illiad, the Æneid, the Divine Comedy, Paradise Lost, and the Nibelungen Lied, as the epics of great nations, it seems incredible that thirty millions of people should cling to a series of moral essays as their typical and honored book. There is no doubt of the fact that the Cural is as essentially the literary treasure, the poetic mouth-piece, the highest type of verbal and moral excellence among the Tamil people, as ever Homer was among the Greeks. We can only explain it by the principle that has so frequently been noted in the preceding pages, that the whole aspect of the Dravidian mind is turned towards moral duty.

There is not one military song in the whole collection that has been made. Nor can any be discovered, except among the Moplas of Malabar. They have many legends of warlike adventure, but their basis is Mahommedan and not Dravidian. The Moplas themselves are followers of the prophet and are a mixed race dating from modern times. The Sepoys of the

British Army are fond of singing the exploits of a certain Rajah of Gingee, but the book is quite modern, and goes no further back than the struggle with the Mahrattas. The poem is not worth translating. Much of the Mahabharata and Ramayanam deals with fighting, but the poems are exotics, nor are the battle scenes those which have caught the public mind.

May we not imagine that it was this moral tendency of the masses which prepared the way for, and maintained the existence of Buddhism. The Brahmans frequently explain the tone of Tiruvalluva, Sivavakyer, Kapila, Auveiyar and the other early Dravidian poets by asserting that they were Jains. There is no proof of this, but it can hardly be doubted that both Buddhism and Jainism reflected the same popular tendency that we see in the early poets. The Brahmans extirpated Buddhism in India by fire, sword and relentless persecution. They could not touch the *fons et origo* from which the rival religion derived its life. By careful avoidance of theological discussion, Tiruvalluva saved his work from the flood that destroyed every avowed obstacle in its grievous course. The Brahmans could find no ground for persecution. No priest can openly condemn the poet who called upon wives to love their husbands; upon men to be truthful, benevolent and peaceful; who enjoined mildness and wisdom on those who governed; and justice, obedience and willing aid on those who were ruled. The Cural says no word against a priest, commands faithful service towards God, paints the happiness of a peaceful home.

Few persons out of the Madras Presidency can have any idea of the reverence and love that surrounds the Cural. Its sentences are counted as binding as the Ten Commandments on the Jews. Its very language has become the test of literary excellence. It is no exaggeration to say that it is as important in Tamil literature, as influential on the Tamil mind, as Dante's great work on the language and thought of Italy. It will not therefore be thought a digression to employ a few pages in sketching the life, legendary certainly but earnestly believed, of Tiruvalluva, the author of the Cural.

It is contained in a book called the Tiruvalluva Charitra. Strangely enough, though the Charitra or Life is in every-day use among the better classes, it is almost unknown to Europeans. I am not aware that it has ever been published or translated except by Monsr. J. Vinson in the Revue Americaine et Orientale, where a French version appeared some years ago. There is also an abstract of the story by Dr. John in the Fourth Volume of the Asiatic Researches. It is well worthy of attention, but all that can be done in these pages is to give a short abstract, dwelling especially on Tiruvalluva's birth and early years.

Brahma desired that the languages of north and south India should be brought to perfection. For this purpose his son Kasyapa took Urvasi to wife, and Vasishtha was born. Urvasi was a *courtesan.* Vasishtha fell in with Arundhati a *chandali* or out-caste woman, and from her Sakti was born. Sakti's son was Parasara, by a *pulæchi* or pariah woman (the word properly means those who eat flesh). Parasara's son by a *valæya* (pariah woman belonging to the fish-eating class) was Vyasa. All of these were learned in the Vedas and brought the northern languages to a high state of perfection.

To perform the same task on the southern or Dravidian languages, Brahma made a Vedic sacrifice. This brought Kaleimagal or Saraswati into existence. Brahma took her for his wife and Agastya was born. He married a daughter of the Ocean, and begot Sagara. Sagara was the father of Bhagavan by a *pulæchi*. Bhagavan was taught all knowledge.

At this time a Brahman named Tapamuni married a Brahman woman, and was the father of a girl. Being about to go on a pilgrimage, it was impossible for him to be troubled with an infant. He therefore left the child by the roadside and thought no more of her. She was found by a respectable pariah belonging to a small town in Mysore, and lived with him for some years. Then the skies rained sand upon the village, and all perished but the little girl. She was mercifully received by a Brahman of Melur, named Nityaya.

Bhagavan, having conquered all knowledge and attained eminence as the holiest of Brahmans, went on a pilgrimage to Benares. On his way he passed through Melur and staid for the night at a chuttrum, or travellers' rest house, near the Brahman village. Having performed his devotions he began to prepare his food.

At that moment the girl came in to see the stranger. He saw at once that she was a pariah, and she did not deny the charge. He became so angry at the pollution she brought that he drove her out with blows and curses. To hasten her departure he struck her on the head with his curry ladle, inflicting a serious wound. The saint went on to Benares, bathed in the Ganges, and after a year or two returned to the south. Again he passed through Melur. Meanwhile the girl had grown into the most lovely of women, beautiful as Lakshmi. Bhagavan caught sight of her and became mad with love. He applied to Nityaya for her hand. The proposal was accepted. The marriage was postponed till Bhagavan's return from Ramēsweram, to whose shrine he was bound to go. On his return the wedding began. On the fifth-day he had to pour oil on his bride's head. To do this perfectly he parted her rich hair with his fingers. This brought to light the mark of the wound. Memory and conscience combined to remind him of his former violence. Struck with double horror, he asked—"Are you the woman I saw before?" Silence proved him right, and he fled from the place. The word *adiyal* means *before*. The question gave the woman a name—*Adi*.

Bhagavan fled all day, but he could not outstrip love. Adi followed and presented herself at the chuttrum where he rested. She refused to be separated and yet live. He was struck with her love, but could not take a pariah. He therefore named a condition that he thought impossible of acceptance—

"If you love me so much, you may on this condition come with me; every child that may be born shall be at once abandoned. Agree to this and you may come." She accepted the hard terms and, unmarried, went with him.

A girl was first born, *Auvei*, or more respectfully Auveiyar. The mother's heart yearned towards the child, and she begged to be allowed to keep it. Bhagavan replied in words that are sacred among the Tamils.

Is that God dead who wrote upon our brow
The things that are to be? Can deepest pain
Be more than He can bear? Doth not He know
Thou hast a child? Let not thy fear complain.

This comforted the mother. She left the little one by the roadside and went on with Bhagavan. The child was found by some temple-singers and was brought up among them as a dancing-girl. She became a famous authoress. The most beautiful of her works is entitled *Attisudi*, and is well worth attention. A portion of it was translated, some years back by the Rev. W. Robinson. His version has been published in the Rev. P. Percival's instructive book,—*The land of the Vedas.*

The next child of Adi and Bhagavan was born in the Tondamandala. It was a girl named *Uppei* or Uppeiyar. Again the mother grew fearful and cried—Who will take care of my little one? Bhagavan replied with the following verse. It will be seen that the birth of each child was the occasion of the composition of a verse, in the metre called *venba.* These verses are now most sacred, and are always quoted with deep reverence. They are probably quotations from some larger work on the Providence of God, which has been lost during the many centuries that have passed since the days of Tiruvalluva.

The king whose pleasure it hath been to feed
All living things, from elephants to ants,
Who ruleth all, hath he forgot our need?
Hath He not taken on Him all our wants?
A mother thou, yet He is still thy God.

This overcame the mother's objections, she left the child behind and went on with Bhagavan. Some washermen found the girl and brought her up as their own. It must be remembered that washermen, though not absolutely pariahs, are the most despised of caste people. To call an enemy a washerman, is to bestow upon him the most deadly insult. The child grew into perfect beauty, and at her death was deified by the common people as Mariamma, the goddess of the Small Pox. She is evidently, from her name, rather the goddess of death. It is hard to see how the beautiful Uppei came to be identified with the dreadful Mariamma. Many hymns of great beauty are ascribed to her.

Bhagavan and Adi wandered into Tanjore, and another child was born at Karuvur, probably the modern town of Caroor. This time it was a boy, who received the name of Adigaman. Again the father reminded Adi of her promise ; again her heart failed her, and she cried—Who will care for my child ?

Bhagavan, for the third time, turned her thoughts to the goodness of God, in the following lines :—

The true and living God knows all our griefs.
He nourishes the egg ere 'tis begot:
He feeds the frog before its rock it leaves:*
If thus He cares for unborn things, will not
He make them grow, when He new life doth add ?
Oh, too distrustful mother, why so sad ?
Rejoice thee in thy God,—give Him the lad.

Comforted by these words, the mother left her son and passed on with Bhagavan. The boy was found and brought to the king of Chēra, who caused him to be instructed in all the learning of the time. Adigamān became a great poet, and recited his most famous work, Ponvannattandādi, at Chillumbrum. His fame reached the heaven of the Gods, who desired to hear him recite and therefore took him to Kailasa at once, without inflicting any subsequent births on him.

Bhagavan and Adi went on to Caverypatam, where another girl was born, named Uruvei. Once more the mother complained of her hard fate, and again Bhagavan comforted her with thoughts of the goodness of God.

* Referring to the fact that frogs are sometimes found imbedded in trees or rocks where, to all appearance, they must have been confined for a long series of years, the poet uses it as a proof of the unceasing care exercised by God over everything that lives.

Hast thou considered what a marvellous thing
It is that life within an egg should dwell?
Or that the food of unborn child should spring
From that which doth its mother's pains dispel?
Why then, Oh mother, art thou so distressed?
Thy God is still a God, by all confessed,
And knowing this thy fears should be repressed.

The child was found by certain charcoal-sellers of the Shanar caste—one of the very lowest in the social scale. She was devoted to God, and became a dancing-girl of the first order. Her accomplishments were very great as, in addition to all perfection in her profession, she was a poet of a high class. Her compositions have perished but not the reputation they brought her. So great was her fame that she accepted a challenge to dance with a God. In that contest she was worsted. After her death she is said to have been deified under the name of Bhadrakali.

Bhagavan and Adi travelled to Trivellore, and in that holy city Kapila was born. The mother grieved to have to lose such a child, but was comforted with the following verse :—

Though God cannot be seen, He knoweth all
Our many needs. He feedeth every day
The frog that on the forest rock doth crawl;
And from our birth till now, hath found a way
To give us day by day our daily food.
If thus it pleaseth Him to do us good
Will not the future bring such plenitude?

Other copies of the book give a similar verse of higher poetic force as the proper utterance on the abandonment of Kapila. As it is deserving of preservation this alternative verse is given—

> Is He that so protected us from birth
> Until this very day, that nothing wrong
> Has ever happed to us;—who made the earth
> Bring forth enough to feed us for so long—
> Hath he now turned from us or doth He sleep?
> Hath His great soul become like thine, to weep
> Where it should joy? Give Him thy child to keep.

Kapila was found by a Brahman, who educated him as his own child, but dared not claim him as a member of his caste. The child grew into a great poet. When he reached manhood, he claimed the privileges of the Brahman. He was denied. His next appeal was backed by proofs of his great poetic power. What was refused to his birth was conceded to his genius and he was admitted into the sacerdotal class. The chief of his works now existing is an *Agaval* or poem in a particular metre. It is especially noteworthy for its attacks on caste. A song that was probably a portion of the Agaval has been inserted on page 168. The poem also contains a short outline of that portion of the Tiruvalluva Charitra which narrates the birth and early progress of Bhagavan's children.

The much tried mother travelled on with the man she loved, and on a mountain in the South another girl was born—Valliyamma. Once more the mother's heart gave way and she cried out in her agony "Who will care for my child?" Bhagavan would not relent, but soothed the stricken woman with the thought—

Will He who placed a living soul in thee,—
Who fed and made it grow within thy womb,—
Will He not feed it still, through life foresee,
O mother, all its wants? Where men entomb
Or burn their dead He danceth without fear.
His head is crowned with serpents; they appear
As if on fire. This God is always near.

The child was found by some members of a jungle tribe known as Kuravers. They are even lower than the Pariahs. The girl was brought up among them, but devoted herself to God. Her genius or penitence was such that the ignorant people venerated her as a deity, and to this day Valliyamma is one of the principal goddesses in the Pantheon of the pagans or ignorant village folk.

Bhagavan and Adi came towards Madras and at Mylapore, one of its present suburbs, Tiruvalluva was born. For the last time the poor mother cried out against the hard lot which compelled her to abandon her child. Bhagavan replied—

Is there or is there not a God whose care
Protects all living things? Have we not life?
Then why, O mother, dost thou flutter here
And cling so fondly to thy babe. Such strife
With God is wrong. On earth all things that are
Are those that ought to be. We may not bar
The course of things, else we God's world may mar.

With this Bhagavan and Adi disappear. Their work was done. Tiruvalluva was left under the branches of a tree, the Bassia Longifolia. For some days no one came near the sacred spot, but the child was nourished by honey which fell into his mouth from the flowers of the tree. At length the wife of a Vellala or cultivator made a pilgrimage to the shrine near which the tree stood. She had no child and yearned for one. A heavenly voice bade her take this boy. She knew it was the offspring of an out-caste, and named it Tiruvalluva, or the holy pariah. She and her husband rejoiced in their adopted son, but the neighbours soon discovered the secret of its discovery or accepted it as a proof of the poor woman's wickedness. They persecuted the unhappy pair so much that the Vellala took the boy to a stable outside the village, that is in the pariah quarter, and arranged with the poor pariahs to bring him up. He continued with them till he was five years old when, learning how much his adoptive parents were maltreated on his behalf, he bade them farewell with many expressions of sorrow, and fled to the mountains, where he dwelt with the holy hermits, and among them was taught all the known sciences and philosophy.

When Tiruvalluva was grown up a fearful monster invaded the plains. He ravaged and destroyed wherever he went and none could withstand his dreadful power. At this crisis a rich landowner proclaimed that to any person who would kill the monster, he would give immense wealth, a whole township, and everything else that might be desired. None dared to accept the task even on such terms. The despairing landowner turned at last to the hermits and asked for such aid as they could give. They too shrank from the task, and only Tiruvalluva dared to attempt it. He was successful. The death of the monster restored peace and prosperity to the whole land. The Vellala landowner was so pleased that he gave the village, wealth and all he had promised, and added the hand of his daughter Vasuki, whom Tiruvalluva married. She proved almost a miracle of goodness, and the songs in the Cural describing the excellency and value of a good wife were confessedly drawn from her life.

Tiruvalluva was now wealthy, but he thought it wrong for any man merely to live, without producing some share of that which he consumed. After careful thought, therefore, he became a weaver. His good wife and he toiled hard at their work, living the while in the performance of every public and private duty. He now gathered many disciples, instructing them in all that concerned holy living. To prove his right to teach he performed many miracles. As his disciples increased they desired that he should make a book in his own name, so that all the world might know how best to live, both in this life and those that were to come. In reply to this repeated request, he sung the Cural in thirteen hundred and thirty verses. He divided it into three parts treating respectively of virtue, wealth, and physical pleasure.

There was then at Madura a college of forty-nine

learned men, who arrogated to themselves the right of deciding finally upon the merits of every literary effort. The legends sometimes say that these poets challenged all the world to equal them or bear their criticism, and that therefore Tiruvalluva humbled their pride ; and sometimes that he desired to hear their judgment and sought them. However this may be, he went to Madura. On the road he met his sister Auveiyar and a contemporary poet of high reputation named Ideikkada, and they went together before the college. There he recited his poem. The savants were astonished but would not at once give way. So they put him a series of questions, which he immediately answered in verses of deep meaning but humorous form.

Still not satisfied, and especially noting that he was but a pariah, who could not be supposed to merit such distinguished honor as their approbation would confer, they said—"O Pariah, a doubt has arisen in our minds concerning the worth of your book, solve this and we will accept it. It is this—the bench we sit on has remarkable power, it will only allow upon it books written in pure high Tamil. So place your book on it. If the bench receive it, we will also." Tiruvalluva accepted the test and placed his book on the bench. The effect was magical. The long bench, that would easily seat fifty persons, began to contract lengthwise. One after another of the judges fell off, until the bench was but just large enough to carry the book and nothing else.

Nothing more could be said. The savants so dreadfully discomfited were honorably free in praise of the Cural. Each man dictated a verse eulogizing the book and its author. These verses remain and are in many cases the sole evidence of the early renown of the writers. Tiruvalluva's glory has never known diminution, and from that day the Cural has been the king of books in the Tamil language.

On his return home, Tiruvalluva went back to his old life, earning with his hands enough for the subsistence of himself and wife, and giving all his wealth away in hospitality. He was once asked which had the greater merit in the sight of God,—a life spent at home in the practice of domestic virtue, or a life apart from men spent in meditation and penance. He decided in favor of the former, but the questioner could not withhold his opinion that Tiruvalluva's excellent wife made all the difference. When she died the glory of his life departed, and though he lived many years after, he never recovered the blow. When his own death was certain, he called his favorite disciple and said,—"The time of my entire perfection is near. When it has come, tie a rope round my body and drag it beyond the limits of the village. Throw it under some bush and leave it there." Then he thanked God that his perfection had so nearly come and, worn out with long and faithful service, lay down and seemed to die. With loving disobedience the disciple prepared a golden coffin, and placed the body within it. But the saint was not dead. Opening his eyes and seeing his surroundings, he said to the disciple—

"What? You have not done what I desired!" With that, it pleased God to take the patient perfect soul to himself. The disciple could no longer disobey. Literally obeying the words of his master he left the corpse under a bush. What wonder filled the people when they saw that the crows and other animals that devoured his flesh became beautiful in outward form and of the color of gold! They erected a temple over the spot and there worshipped the man who had ever taught them to worship God alone.

Now this story is evidently in great measure legendary. Its main object is to prove that Tiruvalluva and all the early Dravidian writers were Brahmans, or at least of Brahman parentage. Adi, the mother of them all, was admittedly brought up as a pariah, but then she was the abandoned child of a Brahman couple. Bhagavan was the son of a pariah mother, as was also his father, and therefore could not have been anything but a pariah himself, but excessive learning overcame this difficulty. Tiruvalluva was confessedly brought up as a pariah, but his powers and learning fully justified his birth and proved him a Brahman after all.

It is as clear as the light that all this is but an example of the literary fraud that has so often been referred to. With Kapila, things were carried further; and his poems were claimed as translations from Sanskrit originals. Popular feeling has prevented the fraud from being completed, for, under Brahman law, connection with a pariah woman is fatal to caste, and this connection tradition compelled the authors of the

Charitra to accept. But the compromise itself suggests that some pariahs in very early times must have occupied a very different position from now. They, or some of the better of them, could dwell in Brahman houses, they could be wives and concubines of Brahmans, the highest means of education were at their service. It probably suggests that the name was then given to classes that are now accepted as Sudras, as for example the weaver castes—Salian and Kaikalar. This has long been suspected by those who have looked into the condition and probable history of the lower Sudra castes. There are the potters for instance. They are known in the caste system as Kosavan, Kumbara, Koravan, &c., and are inferior but acknowledged members of the great Sudra caste. Yet there is a great probability that they are but domesticated (so to speak) members of the jungle race known as Kurubas, Koravers, Kurumbers, &c. Pot-making is the main occupation of both. The pot-maker is an essential member of a society which only uses earthen vessels; and convenience insisted upon his being recognized as a suitable person to deal with and be permitted to live in the village.

The story of Tiruvalluva's weaving probably shows that this was his caste occupation. But this would explain every difficulty, for the weaver may enjoy the privileges the poet received, except that of marrying a Vellala woman. It is of a piece with the history of his mother and grandmother, and would show that, before the castes had time to crystallize, before peace and assured prosperity had made them exclusive, there was much intermarriage that would now be deemed highly irregular.

Strip the story of its Brahmanical element and we learn that Tiruvalluva was a member of a low Dravidian caste, that he attained great celebrity as a poet and as a noble man, that he owed nothing and gave nothing to the sacerdotal caste (after the disappearance of Bhagavan there is not one reference to a Brahman in all the story), and that he was but one of many great Tamil poets who lived about the same time. He probably flourished about the third century of our era.

The Cural is divided into three parts, and contains one hundred and thirty-three pathigams or chapters of ten verses each. The popular reverence it gained from the very first has ensured its preservation, and it is probable that we have it almost unaltered. It has received frequent attention but has never, as far as I am aware, been fully translated into any European language. The third part is, in fact, not suited for a Christian dress. There is, with this reservation, a German translation by Graul in the Bibliotheca Tamulica. The Rev. W. H. Drew translated the first sixty-three chapters into English prose in a masterly way, but died before he could complete the work. Dr. John translated selected portions and published them in the Asiatic Researches. A selection of stanzas from the first thirteen chapters was translated in metre by Mr. F. Ellis, an eminent Madras civil servant. The rendering is exceedingly clumsy, but is the only blot in a most valuable work. It should be admitted, however, that translation was not Mr. Ellis' object, so much as grammatical analysis and the illustration of Tiruvalluva's ideas by parallel passages from other eminent Tamil poets. The abrupt cessation of Mr. Ellis' labors in this direction was a great misfortune for Tamil literature. Isolated chapters, from the pens of missionaries, have occasionally appeared in religious publications. Beyond this I am not aware of any English renderings. Mons. Ariel wrote two learned articles on the Cural in the *Journal Asiatique* in 1848 and 1852, containing translations of many interesting portions, and thus drew considerable attention to the subject in France, but the lead does not appear to have been followed except, more recently, by Mons. J. Vinson, a learned French official at Karikal, who has written several valuable papers on Dravidian literature and language for the *Revue Orientale*.

The following versions have been carefully made and, it is hoped, will give an accurate idea of the style and matter of Tiruvalluva's work. They form about one-eighth of the whole book and one-sixth of the two parts that are adapted to European codes of propriety. For the first three odes, I am indebted to the kind aid of A. W. D. Campbell, Esq., now Head Master of the Bellary Provincial School.

ODES FROM THE CURAL.

PRAISE OF GOD.

As A is the first of all letters on earth,
So is God everlasting of all that hath birth.

The blest feet of the Fount of pure knowledge adore,
Else nought will avail thee, vain pedant, thy lore.

Fast flit those bright feet o'er the flow'r of the mind,
They who clasp them shall flourish, when worlds have declin'd.

At the feet of the Passionless, blessed to rest,
No harm can approach, and no evil molest.

Whoso bringeth to God real homage of heart,
Hath with deeds, the twin offspring of darkness, no part.

Long shall prosper the man that pursues the pure way
Of Him whom the lusts of the senses obey.

If, when sorrows oppress thee, relief thou would'st seek
Fly, fly to the feet of the mighty Unique.

The billows of sin shall not close o'er thy soul,
If thou make but the Ocean of virtue thy goal.

At the feet of the Attributes eight lay thy head,
Else shall it but be as a sense that is dead.

The tide of existence no swimmer can ford,
Save he that doth cling to the feet of the Lord.

Every vernacular book begins with an ascription of praise to some deity. Usually Ganesa and Saraswati are invoked, but Tiruvalluva would have nothing to do with them. His opening chapter is to "The everlasting God." The second song also follows a general custom. Rain is the great requirement of a tropical country. Without it, man and beast must perish. With abundance of rain all nature smiles, plenty fills every garner, poverty becomes bearable for there is the the certainty of food. Most ancient books therefore, follow the invocation of the Deity with the "praise of rain." A collection of these odes would give a very elevated idea not only of the poetical power of the Dravidian people, but of their appreciation of the beneficent operations of nature, and of their perception of the dignity and beauty of the physical world.

THE EXCELLENCE OF RAIN.

'Tis the showers sustain
All nature's domain;
Fit name is Ambrosia for life-giving rain.

'Tis the showers of rain
That produce the grain,
Yield the food that we eat, and the draught that we drain.

If the clouds grudge us rain,
Drought, dearth and their train
Will cause the vast sea-girdled world to complain.

If we get not our rain,
The source of all gain,
Farewell to the plough in the hands of the swain.

The showers of rain
Lay waste the plain,
Then haste to repair their havoc again.

If the clouds withhold rain,
Through the whole champaign
Not a blade of the bright green grass will remain.

Did the clouds not, in rain,
Pay the drops they have ta'en,
They would minish the wealth of the measureless main.

Could mortals no rain
From heaven obtain,
No feasts would they keep; they would brood o'er their pain.

If the sky gave no rain,
Alms, penance were vain,
And soon would mankind abandon the twain.

Without water, would wane
All that earth doth contain;
But there cannot be water, unless there be rain.

VIRTUE.

Virtue can alone bestow
  Bliss above and bliss below:
Say, Oh say, can man possess
  Greater source of happiness?

If to virtue thou take heed,
  Ev'ry good will be thy meed:
Ills unnumber'd overtake
  Those who virtue's path forsake.

Virtue how thou may'st attain,
  Ever strive with might and main:
All thy days to virtue lend,
  All thy pow'rs for her expend.

Where a heart, from sin exempt,
  Prompteth not to some attempt,*
There alone is virtue found:
  All besides is empty sound.

Would'st thou, what is virtue, know?
  All concupiscence forego:
Malice shun; thy wrath restrain;
  Keep thy tongue from words that pain.

Leave not virtue till the last,
  Choose her ere a day be past.
She will be, when death is nigh,
  A support that cannot die.

* This verse will seem obscure to a European, but is full of meaning to the Hindu. When a man knows God, he learns that the wise and infinite Deity has given him all he needs—that he cannot be made happier by striving after worldly fame, wealth or pleasure. His heart therefore should dwell in perfect peace, making no attempt to indulge the senses or gratify the passions.

Needs no diatribe to show
  Virtue's friend and virtue's foe:
Mark who rides along the road ;*
  Note who toils beneath the load.

He that loseth not a day,
  Adding good to good alway,
Is a barrier to impede
  Ages that would else succeed.†

Raptures true from virtue flow,
  Other raptures none can know:
All else, rapture but in name,
  May no panegyric claim.

Whatsoe'er is meet to do,
  That is virtue; that pursue:
Whatsoe'er is meet to shun,
  That is vice, and best undone.

* This couplet is explained by a song already given (Page 169,) where we learn that the present condition of every human being is

"The logical result
Of deeds of good or bad."

The man who rides is being rewarded for patience, justice, toil and faith, either in early life or a former birth. The poor man, who faints in the burning sun under his heavy load, is suffering the due and just reward of his actions. Every act must be worked out. It cannot fail in meeting its reward whether of bliss or pain.

† Repeated births are considered an evil. The very fact that any living soul remains on earth is proof that it has not yet worked off the score against it in the book of God. When by perfect patience, faith, and works, no sin remains unbalanced, the soul suffers no further birth but goes up to God, to be absorbed in Him. Good deeds therefore prevent future births.

THE HUSBAND.

He who is a firm support
  Of the good wherever found,
With domestic bliss is fraught
  And his joys abound.

Household joys shall crown his head
  Who doth aid the helpless poor,
Pays due reverence to the dead,
  Opens wide his door.

Man's whole duty is expressed
  In five-fold service and its cost—
Done to God, himself, his guest,
  Those he loves, and lost.

Sons shall always fill the house
  Where the master shares his food
With the poor; and ne'er allows
  Vice to taint his good.

Love and virtue when combined
  Wedded life to bless and guard,
Show its worth as God designed
  And its great reward.*

* This striking verse might well be adopted as the motto of every home.

He who rules his house in peace,
Making virtue's rule his law,
Hath mighty merit, swift release ;
No recluse hath more.

Thousands strive for future bliss.
'He comes nearest to the goal
Who at home is not remiss,
Blessing every soul.

Swerving not from virtue's path,
Ruling well the household store,
Sheltering hermits by his hearth,—
Penance can no more.*

Marriage is a virtue true:
Marrying not is sometimes right.
But, amongst a world, how few
Can abstain aright.†

Who on earth in wedlock lives
As the strictest duty calls,
Place among the Gods receives,
Rests in heavenly halls.

* This and the sixth verse are hard hits at the sacerdotal system, which makes penance and meditation the highest duties of life.

† How exactly this chimes in with the language of St. Paul! Tiruvalluva is pre-eminently the social poet. In his eyes there is no state of life so pleasing to God as that of the upright, loving, peaceful family. The good husband is better than the most suffering hermit.

THE WIFE.

The wife who excels in the duties of home
  And prudently spends the household means,
Is a help-meet indeed wherever she come,
  Though still in her teens.

The house may be great, may be rich and well known,
  And full of the rarest that money can buy;
Yet all are as nothing if the wife be a drone,—
  Will not even try.

What can that householder desire or wish more
  Who has a good wife to take charge of his folk?
But if she be bad, e'en the richest is poor,
  And death will invoke.

What treasure on earth can compare with the prize
  That falls to the man who obtains a good wife?
As stable and chaste as the lofty blue skies
  She brightens his life.

Each morning adoring her own master and swain,
  Forgetting the God that is greater than he,
She yet so prevails—if she say "let it rain,"
  A storm there will be.*

* So strict a duty is it for the wife to honor her husband that, if in doing this, she forget her God, she shall yet be counted as highly worthy. To honor her husband is to honor God, and therefore the good wife serves the Deity even when she is not aware of it.

Who guards from reproach her own matronly fame,
  And cares for her husband throughout his whole life,
Preserveth unsullied the family-name,—
  She is a true wife.

The guard of a woman is chastity's fence;
  Without it defenceless and shameless is she.
High walls might prevent her departure from thence,
  Yet guilty she'd be.*

The wife that due reverence pays to her lord
  Will reap her reward in the heavens above;
The Gods in their Swerga high place will afford,
  And her they will love.

No husband can walk with a lionlike tread,
  Be bold when his neighbours or foes should revile,
Whose wife has not chastity's mantle o'erspread,
  But selleth her smile.

Good children are jewels adorning the wife
  Who crowneth her husband with loving delight.
Her excellence seizes all causes of strife,
  Withdraws them from sight.

* This verse would seem to show that the modern system of locking women within the house did not then exist. There is every reason to believe that the physical restrain in which Hindu women are so often kept is copied from the Mussulmans, and is but five or six centuries old.

CHILDREN.

In all the world there is no greater good than this—
To have between the knees a son
Whose intellect is bright.

The evils of the seven births shall ne'er be his
Whose sons are free from vice, and shun
The deed that hates the light.

Men call their sons their wealth because they reap in bliss
The good they do the little one
Whose weakness is his might.

The rice in which their child's small hand has played, I wis,
Is sweeter to the parents' tongue
Than could the Gods invite.

What touch is sweeter than our children's loving kiss?
What sound thrills deeper than the tone
Of childhood's wild delight?

"The pipe is sweet, the lute is sweet," say they who miss
The music of their child's hot fun,
When play is at its height.

One mighty good a father gives his children is
To be the best when wise words run
From lips in learned fight.

To e'en the greatest man it cannot be amiss
To joy in that his son has come
Where higher views excite.

The mother when she hears her darling son called wise,
Joys more than when his life begun,
And he first blessed her sight.

That son is good whose life compels the crowed to guess—
" What penance has the father done
To get a son so bright ?"

The last three songs describe the duties of husbands, wives, and children in the family. Those that follow describe our duty to others. Love comes first, for it is the key of every duty, but the poet is earnest in showing that even love becomes an evil unless combined with virtue. The duty of hospitality is insisted on with all the energy of an Arab. Gratitude is extolled in terms that most Christians would deem extravagant. This is the more noteworthy seeing that it has been frequently stated that the Dravidians have no perception of this virtue, because there is no single word in their languages carrying the idea. If the fact were true, the inference would still be wrong. There is no word in the English language for filial love, for a father-in-law, for a metalled road, for an iron-clad vessel, yet it would be absurd to suppose that no such things existed. But it is not the fact, for the simplest school dictionary contains four or five neat renderings of the word gratitude. It is true they are not simple roots but compound words describing the idea. Thus the title of the chapter of the Cural means—recognizing a good that is done. But the English word is of similar character, though not nearly so clear in form. Gratitude comes from gratus, which properly means joyful. Gratus may probably be referred to an earlier form, corresponding to the Greek χαιρω, and this is derived from a root simply meaning rare, valuable. Gratitude therefore means "the joy of receiving." The words gratitude and care show how great the gulf between the original meaning of the root and the present signification of the derivative. The Tamil word is as perfect in form and clear in meaning as the English word telegram. It cannot be too often remembered that the great body of Europeans in India know nothing of Hindu people of the respectable class. Servants are almost invariably pariahs and have nothing in common with the better castes but country and language. That the lowest of the low are given to deceit, fraud and the blackest ingratitude may be true, although it is not admitted as being more deserved than by any other low class, but it is most injudicious and highly unfair to predicate of the respectable class that which has only been observed in the outcast and the ignorant. Let their songs be witness of the sentiments of the middle class.

LOVE.

Can the skill of man devise
  Aught to bar love's sway?
When we would its hopes disguise,
  Tearful eyes betray.

Loveless natures, cold and hard,
  Live for self alone.
Hearts where love abides regard
  Self as scarce their own.

Love and virtue once were wed
  In the days of old,
Soul and body then were bred
  As we now behold.

Love begetteth strong desire,
  Thirst for intercourse.
This createth something higher—
  Friendship's sacred force.

Heaven's happiness, they say,
  Crowns the good above.
It began when virtue lay
  In the arms of love.*

* It should be borne in mind that the "Love" of this ode is almost synonymous with the word "Charity," as found in the standard rendering of St. Paul's Epistles. It is by no means to be confounded with amativeness, or the mutual affection of man and woman.

Vice from love doth often grow,
  Love from deepest sin.
Yet the foolish say they know
  Love is virtue's kin.*

Thus is it when virtue firm
  Hath no loving goal,—
As the sun doth burn the worm,
  So it kills the soul.

In his home the loveless man
  Withers as he lives.
Like a tree beneath a ban,
  Which no stream relieves.

What will active limbs avail,
  Lands or growing wealth,
If no love o'er all prevail
  Giving manly health ?

Where the body hath a soul,
  Love hath gone before.
Where no love infils the whole,
  Dust it is, no more.

* How clear the definition between love and virtue ! Tiruvalluva counts hospitality as one of the chiefest virtues, but, as in this verse, would denounce indiscriminate alms as a vice that grows from love. Compare these remarks of a "heathen" with the new American school that would carry into action the adage that "Love shall still be Lord of all."

HOSPITALITY.

Domestic life, the heaped-up store,
  Should look to one great end,—
To bless the stranger and the poor
  By hospitality.

Though one ambrosia should pour,
  To which the Gods would bend;
To wish a guest outside the door
  Is immorality.

To children's children evermore,
  God doth salvation send,
Of him who daily giveth more
  In hospitality.

Prosperity dwells on his floor
  Who cheerfully doth tend
His guest, and ever proveth pure
  His liberality.

Their fields give increase by the score,
  Though they no seed expend,*
Who eat but what their guests abhor,
  Through hospitality.

* Compare Proverbs xi. 25. "The liberal soul shall be made fat : and he that watereth shall be watered also himself."

The Gods will greet those on the shore
To which the good ascend,
Who having guests, new guests implore,
With true humility.

Who can a kindly deed explore,
Or trace it to its end?
'Tis measured only by the lore
Of hospitality.

"To heap up wealth we laboured sore,
Yet now on gifts depend"—
Say they who from all good forbore
Through lack of charity?*

Amidst their wealth they most are poor
Who ne'er the poor befriend.
Their wealth they only can restore
By hospitality.

The Anicham fades long before
Its sweets you apprehend;
So fares the guest whose host's a boor,
Without civility.

* Compare Proverbs xi. 24. "There is that scattereth, and yet increaseth; and there is that withholdeth more than is meet, but it tendeth to poverty."

GRATITUDE.

A benefit conferred, where none has been received,
Is greater worth than e'er could be achieved
By giving heaven and earth.

And should the gift be made in bitter time of need,
Though it be smaller than the smallest seed,
You cannot weigh its worth.

Who counteth not how great return his gift will bring,
Shall find it weighed by others, as a thing
More heavy than the sea.*

It may be smaller than the smallest seed, and yet,
It is to those who feel its power, as great
As yon palmyrah tree.

* How often do these passages of Tiruvalluva remind of Holy Writ! Compare, for example, this verse with Luke vi. 38. "Give, and it shall be given you; good measure, pressed down, and shaken together, and running over, shall men give into your bosom." I have heard missionaries declare that no other uninspired man, who had not the Bible at his elbow, ever came so near the truth in the higher morality as Tiruvalluva. The first book deals especially with this subject. The maxims of the second book, especially those dealing with the duties of kings, reveal an equal breadth of mind.

We should not measure kindness by its money-cost,
But by the need and worth of those it crossed
When rushing to their end.

Remember all thy life the kindness of the good;
And him who helped thee when thou lackedst food
Count as thy dearest friend.

His love whose hand hath wiped away the falling tear
Can never be forgotten, neither here
Nor in the sevenfold birth.

It is as great a sin to keep a wrong in thought
One moment after, as to count as naught
The gift that saved in dearth.

A single benefit conferred in former time
Will hide, as if in death, a present crime,
E'en though thy blood it spill.

He that hath broken every law of God or man
May yet escape, yet none may 'scape the ban
Who payeth good with ill.

PATIENCE.

How good are they who bear with scorn
  And think not to return it!
They're like the earth that giveth corn
  To those who dig and burn it.

E'en when you can repay in kind,
  Reproach should aye be borne with.
But not to keep the thing in mind
  Is best to repay scorn with.

No poverty so deep as that
  Which leaves the stranger cheerless.
No strength so mighty in combat
  As his whom right makes fearless.

Should you desire to bear for aye
  A name of highest merit?
Then patience should adorn each day
  And exercise thy spirit.

None can esteem a hasty boor,
  Yet all will love the peaceful.
For they are like a golden store,
  So sweet they are and blissful.

Resentful hearts may joy a while;
It will not last the morrow.
But long as earth with flowers shall smile
The meek shall know no sorrow.

Though men should injure you, their pain
Should lead thee to compassion.
Do nought but good to them again,
Else look to thy transgression.

The proud are hateful to their friends,
Offend when they caress you.
Be patient—they will make amends,
Be overcome and bless you.

Ascetics should be holy folk;
But those who bear with rudeness,
E'en when intended to provoke,
Are blessed with far more goodness.

'Tis good to overcome desire,
Abstain from dainty dishes.
To better things thou shouldst aspire;
Endure discourteous speeches.*

* How high the religious state of the man who fifteen centuries ago could write this and the preceding verses. It should be remembered that all the leaders of religious thought among the Brahmans have placed asceticism as the highest of virtues. It is startling to hear a writer whom many would call a "*heathen*" declare that it is nobler and more pleasing to God to be patient under wrong than to spend a life in holy meditation; nobler to endure a discourteous speech than to overcome the physical passions.

BACKBITING.

Though he speak not of right,
And sin with his might,
It is much if 'tis said that he does not backbite.

To deceive with his smiles
The man he reviles,
Is the sin above all which most deeply defiles.

Either here or in hell
In pain he shall dwell,
And receive the reward that the Shasters all tell.

Though you speak to one's face
In words that abase,
In his absence be mindful to speak in his praise.

How empty the mind
Whose praise is but wind!
For see, he reviles when his victim's behind.

All his faults are sought out
And published about,
Who the faults of another delighteth to shout.

He who laughs with a friend
Has friends without end.
If he cannot do this all his words will offend.

If he backbite his own,
The friends he has known,
What will he not do to the poor and the lone?

Were it not for the good
Who vengeance withstood,
E'en the earth would have swallowed the backbiter's brood.

If their faults men but knew
As others they view,
Would the slanderer dare his profession pursue?

Every verse of this ode reminds of some corresponding saying in our own literature. The last verse is a transcript of Burns' immortal lines. The one before it renders literally more than one passage of the Old Testament. The fourth verse anticipated by a thousand years the John Bull adage.—"Say what you like to a man's face but never abuse him behind his back." The sixth and seventh bring to remembrance the saying of our Lord—"Judge not, and ye shall not be judged: condemn not, and ye shall not be condemned: forgive, and ye shall be forgiven."

BENEVOLENCE.

The clouds feed earth with rain,
The earth makes no return.
And thus the good disdain
Rewards that gifts might earn.

To be benevolent
Unto the worthy poor,
Is why all wealth is sent,
And labor addeth more.

Among the Gods above,
Nor in this world below,
Can aught so good as love
Be made with ease to grow.

He only truly lives
Whose charity is free.
But he who never gives
Is dead as dead can be.

The wise his wealth doth bank
By blessing all he meets:
Like streams from brimming tank
Cooling the dusty streets.

A wealthy liberal man
  Is like a fruitful tree,
That ripens in a town,
  Whose fruit to all is free.

With him who knows its use,
  Great wealth is like a plant
Whose bark and leaves conduce
  To cure each dire complaint.

And if their wealth should waste
  The wise will still bestow:
And think that care misplaced
  Which fears what time may show.

The good are only poor
  When naught remains to give.
Then sorrow presses sore,
  They fear 'tis wrong to live.

Some say that gifts are loss:
  Their statement may be true.
'Twere well to bear that cross,
  Though slavery ensue.

INCONSISTENCY.

His very self will laugh aloud
And mock his tortuous path,
Who lives in fraud and lies.

Though high as heaven professions rise,
What can they e'er avail
Against permitted sin?

To be but weak, though seeming strong,
Is like a grazing cow
Dressed in a tiger's skin.

Who hides his sins 'neath saffron robes,
Has but a coward sport
Snaring unwary birds.*

Who falsely say desire has gone,
Will suffer for their sin
And cry—"What have we done?"

* When a man devotes himself to the service of God and becomes an ascetic he either goes stark naked or dresses in yellow from head to foot. This uniform serves him as the cowl and gown of the Franciscan monk, and publishes to all that he is holy. The poet insinuates that they are many who don these robes for wicked purposes. Their supposed sanctity gives them free entry into every house, where silly women and foolish men become their prey, led astray by the idea that ascetics can do nothing wrong.

'Mongst living men the worst are those
  Who cling to darling sin
  Yet seem to shun its stain.

Some men seém fair as coral seed,*
  But in their hearts are black
  As that is at the tip.

How many love to mask their lives,
  Wash clean and seem upright,
  And yet be black as hell!

The arrow kills though flying straight;
  The crooked lute gives joy;†
  Then judge men by their deeds.

If thou abstain from conscious sin,
  There needs no shaven crown—
  No ropes of tangled hair.

* The beautiful scarlet and black seeds of the Wild Liquorice, *Abrus precatorius*, Tamil, *Cundumanni*. The plant grows wild in the Madras Presidency. The fruit is often called coral seed as in the text, because of its brilliant scarlet color.

† Judge not by outward appearances. A man's course may seem direct and straightforward as the course of an arrow, but may only be so consistent because some sin, as fatal to another as an arrow in the heart, is dictating every act. On the other hand, it may seem to us that another man's actions are tortuous and suspicious;—perhaps he is doing good by stealth, perhaps he can only save another from fearful sin by pretending to go part of the way with the sinner, perhaps he is "all things to all men, that he might by all means save some." We must therefore look to the aim or object to be attained, and not simply accept a man for what he at first sight seems to be. We must also remember that we shall be judged by the same law.

THE GOLDEN RULE.

The good are resolved not to injure or hurt, [on earth.
Though 'twould gain them that wealth which brings greatness

Nor will they return of the ill they receive,
Though a foe should inflict an undeserved pain.

If one should do hurt to an unprovoked foe,
He will never escape from the sorrow 'twill bring.

Would you punish the man who has injured your mind?
Oh, put him to shame by your kindness and love.

What good has he gained by his knowledge and skill,
If he strive not for others as much as himself?

No man should consent to inflict or permit
What he knows will give pain to his bitterest foe.

Of virtues the chief—to do nought that is mean,
Though the man may be bad and the time apropos.

Why do men e'er inflict upon others the pain
That experience teaches themselves to avoid?

If a man in the morning bring grief to his foe;
With the eve, uninvited, 'twill come to himself.

To give pain to another brings ten back again.
Would you guard you from grief? To another cause none.

MALAYALAM SONGS.

It has already been stated that the Malabar Coast exhibits in its highest form the metamorphic effect of Brahmanism. Dravidian literature scarcely exists, and the language itself is so overborne with Sanscrit words that it sounds more like a Prakrit than a Dravidian tongue. The legend of Parasurama is doubtless an exaggerated description of a real Brahmanic conquest, in which the early peoples were entirely trodden down and their nationality well nigh extinguished. Hence the land can scarcely be said to have a literature at all. Sanscrit works are numerous but are evidently foreign. Early Dravidian literature perished in the storm of conquest. Malayalam literature has scarcely begun. The Brahmans scorn the mongrel tongue that is the badge of inferiority. The lower castes have lost the key, as it were, of national composition. Sanscrit is the learned language, but no Nair or Tier may learn it. Few Nairs will write in Malayalam, for then no Brahman will care for it, and to the masses it would be strange.

It is probably not incorrect to say that there is no pure Malayalam literature extant that dates from more than a few centuries back. The earliest poem is the Rama Charitram, but its very name proves its Sanscrit origin, although its age makes it interesting. Then follow, but long afterwards, translations of the Ramayanam, Mahabharata and the Puranas. The Kērala Utpatti, local in its character and therefore characteristic of the country, more nearly approaches to what we might call national literature; but it is a historic legend of purely Brahmanic interest.

It has been a matter of great difficulty to discover any thing that could be called a folk-song between the Western Ghauts and the sea, and the following are offered with some diffidence. They were popular lyrics, and still fly from mouth to mouth in Malabar and, so far, are certainly folk-literature. But they are antique in language, probably the remnants of a fading class of poetry, and are evidently less known now than they were a century ago. Notwithstanding their age they are not Dravidian, for, as will be seen, they are purely puranic, deal only with the Brahmanic deities and are based altogether on the Bhagavatam and the modern pantheon. Hence it is clear they are not Dravidian, in the sense that they do not belong to the soil. They are popular adaptations of a foreign theme.

Except the last, a riddle, the songs are all amorous. This of itself is sufficient to stamp them as importations. The first is very curious as showing how easy it is to make the step that separates the sublime from the ridiculous. It is a domestic quarrel between God and Goddess reduced to homely language, and thus shows how much like naughty men and women, naughty deities may be. It is a dispute between Krishna and his wife Radha. The latter is jealous, and according to the Puranas had abundant reason to be so. How modern it all seems! Yet the classical scholar will at once say—how old it all is! The Hindu deities are so much like the old Greek ones, in conduct and speech, that nothing seems altered but the names. But let us hear the Gods themselves.

IRÆ AMANTIUM.

KRISHNA.

O thou who art most beautiful,
  The daughter of the mountain king,
Art thou asleep or lying down,
  Hearing not my call?

How long have I been waiting here
  Detained from love and highest joy!
Thou art my sweetest counsellor.
  Open then the door.

RADHA.

What ails thee, Hari? Tell me first
  Where thou hast stayèd out so late?
If Jagganatha* tells me this
  He shall wait no more.

* Jagganatha is one of the thousand names of Krishna and means "Lord of the Universe."

KRISHNA.

Great Vishnu praised me, Indra too;
I staid while they did worship me,
And hence am late. So let me in.
This is not a lie.

RADHA.

How many lies a God can tell!
I will not ope the door, for I
Can smell perfumes, can see the ash,
Telling of thy sin.

KRISHNA.

I tell you but the truth, yet you
Think me a liar. I am pained
That you should doubt me. Open then:
Let me enter now!

RADHA.

How shamefully you would deceive
Your honest wife! But I know all
Your pranks with Gunga.* With the morn
I will ope the door.

KRISHNA.

Why charge me thus, my lovely one?
I burn with love for thee. Thy darts
Have pierced me through. Open the door:
Else for love I die.

* The river Ganges is personified in the Puranas as a lovely woman, Gunga. She sprung from Vishnu's head, and her beauty won his love.

RADHA.

Oh, master, can I meet thy craft?
  When you have told me why you come
At midnight, I will let you in.
  Now the doors are shut.

KRISHNA.

Why say such things? It is no lie.
  No other woman shares with thee
The love that sets my heart on fire.
  Do not shut me out.

RADHA.

Your very words betray your fault:
  You *have* been visiting the quean.
If God himself should order me,
  Open I will not.

KRISHNA.

Why say so many nasty things?
  My heart doth burn; I'll kiss thy feet;
Will bow before thee to the earth;
  If thou let'st me in.

RADHA.

Her heart did melt at last. She cried—
  Come in, come in, my husband dear!
The door is open. Ere 'tis day
  Joy may fill our souls.

The next is addressed to Parvati, the consort of Siva, under the name of Kali. She represents in Southern India the Durga of the north and the Bhavani of the books. She is not exhibited as the horrid monster which takes the name of Durga ; but is a well-formed beautiful woman, whose aspect only becomes terrible when engaged in ridding the world of such monsters as Darrika and Mahishasura. She represents the *Sakti* or creative power, and is therefore properly described as the giver of all good things, the bestower of joy, the provider of daily food. The song deserves attention, further, in that it forms the first prayer and utterance of thousands of people each day. It is the morning hymn of the Sakti Saivas in Malabar.

MORNING HYMN TO KALI.

Oh beautiful one, who laughest so low,
Amusing thyself with Kama's great foe,*
Praised be thou.

Thou givest all joy, with pleasures dost crown
Who worshippest thee, at thy feet bowing down.
Praised be thou.

Old Indra reveres, the Munis adore
The Goddess we praise, whose grace we implore.
Praised be thou.

* When Kama, the God of love, was plaguing Siva one day with his shafts, Siva became angry and consumed Kama with one fiery glance. He was restored to life, but never fully recovered from the effects of Siva's wrath.

Thou art, as it were, the key of the earth;
The mother of all, we owe thee our birth.
Praised be thou.

When hunger attacks, the heat of midday,
Thou givest us food, fatigue flies away.
Praised be thou.

Thou tookest with ease great Darrika's head;
Relieved all the world by leaving him dead.
Praised be thou.

How mighty thou wert, how fierce in the fight,
When Mahishasura was slain by thy might!
Praised be thou.

Yet art thou so meek, thy temper so bland,
That Brahmans are fed with rice from thy hand.
Praised be thou.

Thou givest each day thy blessings in heaps,
Removest alarms; thy love never sleeps.
Praised be thou.

Oh goddess, grant me thy beauty to see!
I worship thee now. From sorrows set free.
Praised be thou.

Each day ere the light I crave for thy grace,
And offer this prayer before thy sweet face.
Praised be thou.

Who daily repeat it, who hear it each morn,
Shall always have food, their barns shall have corn.
Praised be thou.

The song is of such interest that a freer and more spirited version by Mr. C. M. Barrow, the able Head Master of the Calicut Provincial School, may not be thought out of place. It has not been previously published and was written for this book.

1. All praise and worship be to thee,
Thou beautiful, that merrily
With Kama's foe doth play;
Thou who dost bless with pleasure those
Whose souls in Thee their trust repose
Throughout the livelong day.

2. To thee, O Princess, chastely bright,
Let praise and worship with delight
By all the gods be given.
To thee, O mother of us all,
Who dost our very hearts enthral;
Who hold'st the keys of heaven.

3. From those whose hearts with toil are faint,
Their strength in midday labour spent,
Whom hunger home doth drive,—
Let thanks for aye to thee up go,
To thee who kill'd'st *our bitter foe* ('Darika)
With whom no more we strive.

4. To thee, O fierce and full of fame,
Who *Earth's strong enemy* (Mahishasura) didst tame
When he thy might withstood.
To thee let all give daily praise,
For thou the Brahmins' hearts dost raise
By sending holy food.

5. Be praised, O goddess, evermore,
Since thou on men thy good dost pour
And tak'st away alarms.
May I thy form's divinest grace
With purgèd eye see face to face,
And gaze upon its charms.

6. To thee apart my prayer I make,
My daily woes away to take,
For thee my soul doth crave.
Oh goddess, let thy presence bless
My nights and days. By holiness
Do thou thy suppliant save.

7. To those who offer up this prayer
Devoutedly, at morn and eve,
Of all good things, O goddess, give
A full and an abundant share.

The next two songs are in honor of Krishna. They dwell with marked emphasis on his peccadilloes, but find in them reasons for new love; much as a long suffering mother expends her deepest affection upon the scapegrace who brings shame upon himself and all belonging to him. Krishna is emphatically the *pet* of the people—the merry ne'er-do-well who, when occasion requires, is the bravest of the brave; and who, all over the world, wins the hearts of men and women. He is the incarnation of the lusts of the flesh and the pride of life; never turning from temptation, never thinking of the future.

KRISHNA.

---

1. Krishna killed ten kings:
   I worship him.
   Born to bear our load:
   I worship him.
   Necklaced, bright with rings:
   I worship him.
   Krishna, purple-robed.
   I worship him.

2. Ghee and milk he stole:
   I worship him.
   Poothana he killed:
   I worship him.
   All at once his soul:
   I worship him.
   With love's darts was thrilled.
   I worship him.

3. Child of God, of truth the ark:
   I worship him.
   Wearing belt and rings of gold:
   I worship him.
   Tending kine in jungles dark:
   I worship him.
   Lion of the earth of old:
   I worship him.

4. Man and lion all in one:
I worship him.
Skilled in war, whose arrow keen,
I worship him.
Ere its lightning course was done,
I worship him.
Seven great palm trees cleft in twain.
I worship him.

The "Lament for Krishna" is put in the mouth of Krishna's foster mother, Yasoda the wife of Nanda, the cowherd who saved young Krishna's life and brought him up as his own son. It ascribes to Krishna the title Narayana, which is properly the most honorable name of Vishnu in his divine form. As Krishna was an incarnation of Vishnu this ascription is not improper. The references in the song are all to incidents in the life of Krishna as given in the Vishnu Purana, Gita Govinda and Bhagavatam, and do not need comment.

It must be remembered that the Krishna of the Mahabharata is a very different being from the Krishna of the Gita Govinda. It is a common saying among the Hindus.—"If you want true manliness, look to Rama; if you want to please the women, look to Krishna." But the Krishna of the epic is as noble a being as Rama. He is the greatest of warriors, the wisest of sages, the divinest of teachers. In the Bhagavat Gita we find Krishna's highest expression, and in the Gita Govinda his lowest.

LAMENT FOR KRISHNA.

1. Oh, Narayana! My soul is weak
   Within me, for nowhere can I see
My lotus-eyed one. Is he sick,
   Or has he hurt his arm or knee
While stealing butter-milk and curd?
                    Oh, Narayana!

2. Have robbers carried him apart,
   Lest he should tell they stole the kine?
Deep sorrow overwhelms my heart.
   I cannot see my son divine,
Whose hair is dressed in glossy braids
                    Oh, Narayana!

3. My heart is broken if he stay
   Away from me. His smiling face
Must shine upon me, as the day.
   Has he been frightened in the chase,
And ran he knew not where for help?
                    Oh, Narayana!

4. Oh! Has he fled to jungles dark
   Escaping dreadful present ill?
Has hunger made him eat the bark
   Or fruit of forest trees, that kill
All those who taste the tempting food?
                    Oh, Narayana!

5. He is not given to go away:
E'en when he lost his tinkling chains
And flute, he did not go astray.
He must be listening to the strains
That flow from cowherds' simple pipe.
Oh, Narayana!

6. But now I see him! I am shod
And crowned with gladness. I will run
To care for him. But, oh my God,
Let not the loss of such a son
Bring desolation to my home!
Oh, Narayana.

We cannot better close this small collection of Malayalam songs than with the following riddle. It is a good example of a class of composition that holds a high place in the lower literature of some of the Dravidian tongues. They are propounded with the utmost gravity in assemblies that, according to our views, ought to be the last to give way to pranks of this sort. But every man to his taste, and nation too. The propounding and solution of good riddles is no mean intellectual amusement. The key of the riddle is the word *naiva*, the tongue. It is composed of two syllables, each of which is sometimes an independent word. The first syllable, *nai*, is a dog. The second syllable, *va*, is the imperative of the verb to come.

A RIDDLE.

I am very old.
When the first man was,
I was there with him.
Ancient kings thought me
Best among their friends:
Me they worshipped oft.

I sing praise to God
And have long done so.
God gave me a house,
Where I live on earth.
Yet he gives to all
What he gave to me.

Round my house are built
Mighty palisades,
Keeping out my foes.
Outside these again
Is another wall,
Guarding me from hurt.

Like raw meat I seem,
Yet am well and strong.
When my friends are sick,
I am out of health.
Sometimes I get sick
Then my friends are ill.

Members two have I.
Guess my first, I pray.
When my last comes forth,
Seems as if a man
Called an idle slave.
When my whole is said
Dogs collect in crowds,
Running fast and long
Lest they be too late.

TELUGU SONGS.

Of the greater Dravidian languages there remains but the Telugu, the sweet sonant tongue of the people between the Rivers Palar and Mahanuddy. It has been very justly styled the Italian of the East, and for flexibility and fullness may worthily compare with Greek. Although not nearly so much Sanscritized as Malayalam it is yet the best vehicle for Sanscrit sounds and compound words, and hence has arisen a great mass of literature transliterated from Sanscrit into Telugu. This is made bearable and possible by the fact that the Telugu speech runs parallel with Sanscrit in its sandhi or mode of forming compound words, its collocation of words in the sentence, and its general grammatical structure. Not that there is any suspicion that Telugu is derived from Sanscrit. Far from that. Like the sister languages, Tamil, Canarese, Tulu, &c., Telugu is Aryan, and derived its source from the great fountain of which Sanscrit and the Dravidian group are but branching streams. But more than the other members of the group it retains that hereditary force which renders hybridism possible. Thus Sanscrit verbiage runs easily in Telugu letters.

This facility of transliteration has done much harm to Telugu. Sanscrit words were so easily borrowed that borrowing became a habit; not, it is true, to the destruction of the national vocabulary as in Malayalam, but to the overloading of it. This process would inevitably have led to an utter change of the national tongue as Brahman influence extended, had not the English conquest intervened and compelled Sanscrit to enter the lists against a most active and penetrating foe. Besides this, large portions of the Telugu country are even yet unknown to the Brahmans, who have only settled in the richest provinces and along the coast; and thus there has always been a spring of Telugu, pure and undefiled, to well over the land and save the country tongue from destruction.

Another cause has, however, done tenfold more damage to Telugu people's literature; that is, foreign conquest. The traveller through Telugu districts is constantly coming on the tokens of former magnificence. Temples falling to pieces, ruined cities, mouldering pillars, abound everywhere and tell of wonderful wealth and power in ages now forgotten. Amravati is but one of a hundred such. But a few years back the great territory of Gondwana was marked on the maps as "unexplored territory," so desolate was it, so given over to barbarism and all unfruitfulness. Yet in the midst of ancient jungle, buried among the mighty trees that crown the hill tops, are the remains of gigantic cities that must once have buzzed with the noise of a hundred thousand people.

History fails to tell us much of what these kingdoms did, whom they conquered, how they fell. But geography steps in to prove how far their arms reached;

how deep the impress they left. All over the Indian seas we find the tokens of a great Telugu dominion. What are the Klings of the Malay peninsula, but Kalingas, a branch of the great Kalinga or Telinga nation? Who built the monster temples of Sumatra, Java and the Archipelago, whose towering summits still point to the heaven of Swerga? No other people than the Telugus, the Phœniciens of the Indian ocean. In Burmah and Siam are the footprints of the same people.

But we need not leave India to learn the same story. The Dara Kumara Charitra, dating from the tenth century, speaks of the Telugu kingdom of Andhra as if it were a great maritime power, with fleets of ships of war and sailors by thousands. Probably the references may belong to a much earlier period; and in any case we know that the great Telugu conquests across the sea were made much earlier. What are the Kavarai, the Vadukan, the Velamas of Southern India, from Mysore to Cape Comorin, but Telugu settlers, whose social position and landed property still proclaim them as conquering tribes, the outposts of the Telinga kingdom?

The last of the great Telugu kingdoms was that of Vijianuggur. It was supreme in Southern India from about 1300 to 1600, A.D. Before the rise of this state, the great Belal kings ruled at Warunkul. Before these were the Cadumba and Chalukya dynasties, the latter of which reaches back into dim antiquity before the Christian era. In the time of Pliny or, rather, in the still earlier days of the writers whom Pliny trusted, the Telugu kingdom was supreme,—a civilized mighty state ruling over the Eastern coast of India from the Ganges to the Cauvery. From the overthrow of the kings of Vijianuggur to the rise of the British ascendency under Warren Hastings, confusion and despair fell upon the poor Telugus. *Ichabod*, the glory is departed.

Moguls, Pathans, Mahrattas, Pindarries and Mysoreans, Nizams, Soubahdars and Rajahs came like waves over the rich land. Perhaps the strength of the nation had gone to foreign parts and the home-stayers were too weak to fight, but whether this were so or no, the Telugu nation was nearly wiped off the face of the earth. There came to it what fell on Tyre and Carthage, the homes of its antetypes in the Mediterranean. Where once dwelt a great nation now roam the wild tribes of Bustar and the hill agencies. Human sacrifices are offered where once ambassadors were received.

In this great destruction the people's literature could not survive. There is scarcely a Telugu book older than the thirteenth century, and only the Telugu Mahabharatam and the grammar of Nunniah Bhutt were, in their present condition, written earlier than the twelfth century. But even these do not represent the people's ideas, for they were all written by Brahmans for Brahmans. Campbell broadly states that the "intolerant zeal of the Mahomedans......has left of the more ancient Telugu works little else remaining than the name." And again—"Indeed the three inferior classes of

Telingana......seem to have abandoned the culture of their language, with every other branch of literature and science, to the sacred tribe. The Vussoochuritru is the only Telugu work of note not composed by a Brahmin."

There is but one slight error in this description—the omission in the last sentence of the work of Vemana. Compiled, according to Mr. Brown, in the sixteenth century, this is just the work we require. Vemana was probably the arranger rather than the author of the thousands of quatrains of purely popular lore which go by his name. Very far below Tiruvalluva in moral feeling, and still further away in poetic power, Vemana is yet more useful in exhibiting popular ideas; for he gathers what previously existed, while Tiruvalluva made what became the national heritage. Whether Vemana found them or made them, the quatrains are now the proverbial stock of the people. Any one may be quoted independently. Scores of them are contradictory, a fact that makes it almost certain that Vemana did not make them all. As far as is now known, this long chain of unconnected verses is the only great remnant of Telugu folk-lore,—purely national, strongly monotheistic, intensely vulgar, using the word in its proper sense. It is interesting to note how exactly the verses chime in with all that has gone before. With the single exception of the inhabitants of the Malabar coast, we find all the Dravidian nations preaching the same truth, serving the one God, hating the Brahmans.

We are absolutely ignorant of the life of Vemana and of the date of his birth or death. Mr. C. P. Brown, the greatest of living Telugu scholars, thinks that he lived in the sixteenth century, but this is confessedly a mere guess. Mr. Brown's opinion is based upon the character of the language of the book that goes by his name and the local references that seem capable of identification. But it is certain that the book has been again and again revised; and the modern marks referred to would in all probability be due to the revisor. Mr. Brown has omitted to note that certain passages of the book explicitly state that Vemana wrote at an earlier date. The following are quoted from Mr. Brown's translation:—"In this iron age has Vemana by his celebrity rendered the farmer tribe honorable; striving to attain to the Supreme God, he has dealt forth to all men, every truth he knew."—"Incessantly did Vemana speak in our ears, saying, evident and manifest is the deity; be wise, attain it, and be for ever happy!"—"Verily the foolish wretches, who are unable to comprehend the mental wisdom taught by Vemana, shall perish like a hair when separated from the head; devoid of sustenance here and perfection hereafter."

All these, and there are many like them, imply that Vemana wrote at a much earlier date and that, therefore, if the book in its present form is to be referred to the sixteenth century, Vemana himself lived long before. From the absence of reference to Mahommedanism and the Moslem rule, and the close resemblance in style and matter to the Tamil poets of the tenth century or thereabouts, it is suggested that the proper date of Vemana's life is not later than the end of the twelfth century. Certain passages in the book would seem to show that he was a jangam or priest of the Lingayet or Vira Saiva sect. But even this is not otherwise known. The only direct statements are that he was born from Velama or cultivator parents, and that he was a yogi or hermit. But this latter point is clearly contradicted by the numerous passages that ridicule the yogi and place meditation very far down in the list of virtues.

There can, however, be little doubt that the bulk of the sayings are older than their reputed author, and have been floating among the common people for many centuries. Vemana probably added very many of his own. But it is extremely doubtful whether Vemana ever saw more than half of the epigrams that go by his name. Mr. C. P. Brown, to whose version of a selection of about seven hundred of the quatrains I am greatly indebted, and whose literal prose translation is the base of the renderings that follow, made a large collection of MSS. going by the name of Vemana, but none contained more than eight hundred verses, while most exhibited not more than three or four hundred. The collation of the MSS. revealed more than two thousand distinct epigrams. It is exceedingly improbable than any work so important as that would have been which should have contained the two thousand verses, could have been so broken up as the versions now are, without exhibiting some sign of the process in the way of grouping or acknowledged selection. But this we do not see, at least to any extent.

On the other hand, nothing is more likely than that the success of Vemana's genuine collection of proverbs should have led imitators to make similar gatherings in their own locality. The more widely-known proverbs entered into several collections. The very easy metre of Vemana's work made the task a simple one, and hence the present series is probably a sort of *olla podrida* of Telugu folk-sayings cast into metrical form. This will not detract from the value of the book for our purpose, but rather increase it, since the popular character of the epigrams is the more certain.

It has been stated that the verses of Vemana exceed two thousand in number. They follow in no order, but are jumbled together; as if each verse had been written on a card, all the cards tossed together in a bag, and then the cards withdrawn at random and strung together in the order in which they came from the bag. The following versions are groupings of quatrains of similar subject, and it must be understood that, though they are faithful renderings, they do not, in sequence, at all follow the original.

OBSERVANCE OF RITUAL.

To pray and serve yet not be pure,—
In dirty pot to place good food,—
To worship God while sins endure,—
Can never turn to good.

Our sins grow ever from our deeds,
Nor owe their birth or death to place.
'Tis better, then, to see our needs
Than look to works for grace.

Why dost thou long for holy springs,
Or seek at Kasi saintlihood?
Can sinful man obtain the things
That Kasi gives the good?

Though hypocrites should meditate,
And perfect keep the outward law,
They ne'er attain the holy state;
But sink in hell's dark maw.

The sanctity that God counts right
Is not in sky or deserts rude;
'Tis not where holy streams unite:—
Be pure—thou viewest God.

God looks not on our race or dress,
But dwelleth closely with the soul;
And those who don strange garb would bless
Their bellies with your dole.

This quickly dying flesh to please
  Most men will bear perpetual pain;
They will not risk a moment's ease
  Eternal bliss to gain.

What fools the pilgrims are who think
  That God may not be found at home.
'Tis exercise alone. They sink
  In woe: then back they come.

With eager mind they see Sathu,
  Prayaghi, Kasi, Madura
And Kanchi. What can all these do?
  'Tis naught but walking far.

To feed the hungry and the poor
  Is nobler deed than sacrifice.
What greater good can man procure
  Than save the poor from vice?

Some mortify their flesh and take
  The name of saints; yet cannot cleanse
Their hearts. Will you destroy the snake
  By scraping its defence.*

The sacrifice that fools lift up
  Is never perfect, brings no profit.
The dog that tries to lift a cup
  Will damage it or drop it.

* Alluding to the common fact that snakes will take up their residence in the ready-made holes of deserted ant-hills, he points out that to scrape the out-side of the ant-hill will not kill the snake that dwells within it. You may make the ant-hill look nice, but it is as dangerous to approach as ever.

RITUAL NOT RELIGION.

Will seeing Concan make a dog a lion?
Or Kasi make a pig as great
As any elephant? How then
Can they a saintly man create?

Though he should daily read or hear
The Veds, the sinner still is vile.
Will not its blackness still appear
Though coal in milk be washed a while?

Thy creed and prayers may both be right,
But see that truth marks every plan;
Else thou shalt never see the light.
The truthful is the twice-born man.*

The fount of happiness is in
The heart. The foolish man confides
In man! He's like the stupid swain
Who seeks the lamb his bosom hides.†

* Over and over again do we find passages asserting that the new birth which makes a Brahman adult "twice-born" must be a moral change if it would be accepted by God. They assert not only that new birth must represent a moral change but that the truly good man is sure to experience the conversion.

† This refers to a common story of a stupid shepherd who went everywhere searching for the lamb that he was, all the while, carrying in his bosom, because it was too weak to walk. It corresponds to the English saying of the man who looked for the spectacles that were perched above his nose.

Religions counted by the score
  There are. But yet not one is good
If faith be lacking in its lore.
  Faith makes our worship please our God.

The dog doth love midst trees to go,
  The crane stands still, the ass brays chants,
The frog bathes oft.* Can yogis know
  The heart of man with all its wants?

They read the Shasters, write them out,
  And learn the truths that in them lie.
And yet of death they are in doubt:
  They know not even how to die!

You smear your face and arms with ash,
  Hang silver idols round your neck!
All this may help to swell your cash,
  But in the coming world will wreck.

"Thou art unclean! O, touch me not!"—
  They cry. But who can draw the line?
What man was born without a spot?
  In each man's flesh sin has a shrine.

* To live in the forest, to stand perfectly still in deep meditation, to chant in a loud monotone the name of the Deity, and to take every opportunity of ceremonial bathing, are the marks of a Hindoo saint. He is the greatest saint who can stand motionless the longest, chant the thousand names the loudest, &c. The epigram points out that certain despised animals can excel the highest saint in exercises of this sort.

IDOLATRY.

What animals ye are who worship stones
  And care not for the God that dwells within!
How can a stone excel the living thing
      That praise intones?

And how can those who serve a carved rock
  Bow down before and praise the living One?
Can he who tastes the honey on his tongue
      Rank poison suck?

What strange delusion draws your mind to dream
  That God doth dwell in senseless images?
Is broken stone, which neither hears nor sees,
      Fit house for Him?

Yet men take earth, make idols, set the clod
  In honor, count as gods and worship them!
How can they dare so blindly to contemn
      Their inward God?

Why bow and fall before the idol's throne?
  The stone will not be changed. But ken
That God dwells in the soul. Why then
      Adore a stone?

The man that fasts shall next become a pig:
  Who bows before a stone a stone shall be:
And he who wrongly chooses poverty
      Shall have to beg.

What fools! They take a stone from off the hill,
  And after knocking it about with hands and feet,
With chisels cut it and with hammers beat:
      Then chants they trill.

The living useful bull you starve and beat;
  But when 'tis carved in stone you it adore!
How gross such sinful folly is! Abhor
      So clear a cheat.*

Around a mould of wax you stick some clay;
  Then melt the wax, and in its room instal
Some melted metal. This your God you call
      And serve each day.

While He, the worshipful, dwells in the heart,
  Why pile your gifts in temples made of stone?
Can gods who, in and out, are rock alone
      E'er taste a part?

* This verse hits one of the greatest blots in the Hindoo character. Kine have to serve for all the purposes that, in Europe, fall to the lot of horses. They are, therefore, constantly urged to tasks beyond their power. When they resist or fall down, the most cruel punishments are inflicted. There is not one bullock out of six whose tail has not been dislocated, while many animals have suffered dislocation of almost every joint. For the meres tailment the most extensive branding will be prescribed, and sickly bullocks show brands that equal the tattooing of a South Sea islander.

CASTE.

If we look through all the earth
  Men, we see, have equal birth.
Made in one great brotherhood,
  Equal in the sight of God.

Food or caste or place of birth
  Cannot alter human worth.
Why let caste be so supreme?
  'Tis but folly's passing stream.

While the iron age doth last,
  Men are good in every caste.
Blustering fools all men despise;
  None are good in such men's eyes.

Viler than the meanest race
  Is the man before whose face
Others only Sudras are.
  Hell for him shall ne'er unbar.

Empty is a caste-dispute:
  All the castes have but one root.
Who on earth can e'er decide
  Whom to praise and whom deride?

Why should we the Pariah scorn,
  When his flesh and blood were born
Like to ours? What caste is He
  Who doth dwell in all we see?

DEATH.

All those who brought us forth are not,
And most of those whom we begot.
Is this not proof enough? Shall we
Live long as God's eternity?

Before the spirit goes, 'tis right
To use all means to keep alight
The vital flame. But when away,
What use to try its flight to stay?

The rich man dies; his stores remain.
When he returns, he has again
To earn, and, dying, loses all.
Where then his wealth and where his soul?*

For naked every man was born,
And naked must he die. Forlorn
He roams the earth, is naked still:
For good he cannot do or will.

* This verse gives, very tersely, one of the principal complaints of the people against transmigration. Human labor is like that of Sisyphus,—it is always beginning again. I believe this palpable vanity of earning is one of the greatest temptations to ascetic life that a Hindoo can meet. Surely it is very hard of God, they say, not to permit a man to begin his second life at the point where he finished his first. How can he profit by experience, how acquire the necessary merit, if he must always begin afresh as ignorant, as poor, as helpless, as when he began the life of which he made such a failure, and which he now must expiate?

If iron break it needs repair,
  The smith can weld again as fair.
But if the spirit break and fail,
  Who then can it restore or heal?

If chatties break, we new ones buy.
  If then a living man should die,
What wonder that his soul should get
  Another body for its seat!

The holy saint whose course is run,
  Shall in the world above the sun
Perceive and really know and see
  The Formless, crying—"This is He."

However long we live or learn,
  However great the fame we earn,
We live at best but one short day.
  With all our skill we turn to clay.

The brutish man counts as his own
  The wealth of all his house. Alone
He buries it.* Yet when he dies,
  Not e'en a pice with him he hies.

* It is certain that the universal peace and justice that came in with the British is fast overcoming the habit of burying all superfluous cash and valuables. Vemana constantly refers to the practice, not to condemn its propriety from a business point of view, but to urge that it would be much better to give to the poor that which cannot be used. Such liberality may make the money-gainer less wealthy here, but goes a very long way to prevent the burying of the giver in a score of 'troublesome births.' Supreme felicity may be earned by perfect liberality.

What are our wives, our sons, our friends,
And what relations' love, when ends
This life? Can we on slaves rely?
Not one can help us when we die.

Our body, like an earthen bowl,
Will surely die. But still the soul
Lives on. Many pots may go,
But none the less the waters flow.

How great the folly tears to shed
When friends depart! "Oh, he is dead,"
"Oh, he is dead," they loudly cry.
As if a living soul could die!

While health is good they live in lust;
When death draws near to penance trust.
How can they dream of swift release
While yet the heart is not at peace?

He that is wise shall live for aye.
When earth breaks up his soul shall stay
Unhurt. When all things else are gone,
His soul shall join the mighty One.

MORALS.

Except when duties call,
  Forget thy lordlihood.
The low may yet be good.
  A glass makes mountains small.

Forgive thy conquered foe:
  For thus your foe you kill;
Thy love his hate will still.
  Then let him freely go.*

Who gives, yet covets not,
  Who shuns his neighbour's wife,
Shares not in angry strife,
  Is wise and hath no spot.

Good deeds that pure hearts do,
  Though small, are great in meed:
How tiny is the Banyan seed,
  How great a tree doth grow!

Gifts merit thanks not small,
  But meditation more;
By wisdom higher soar;
  Pure hearts are best of all.

* Compare this verse with the stanzas of Tiruvalluva's on Page 236, fourth verse, and Page 238, second verse, and both with our Lord's command —"Love your enemies, do good to them that hate you, and pray for them which despitefully use you." Many passages strongly remind of the Cural, and it is quite possible that they were originally derived from it, since it is well known that the Cural was exceedingly popular long before the twelfth century, and nothing is more likely than that the conquering Telugu armies should bring back with them the poetry as well as the spoils of the Tamils.

Thy words, Oh God, are mine;
  Thy house is my abode:
My thoughts in thine are showed;
  My joy shall copy thine.

The good adorn our globe;
  Beneath them are the proud.
But those are worst who shroud
  Their greed neath saffron robe.

We see the truth in Thee,
  In us delusion hides.
But when the Godhead guides,
  Ourselves aright we see.

By seeking we find Him;
  He seeketh those who seek.
Alas, how few awake
  To seek their God in time.

He loveth those who love:
  Who love Him not He spurns.
False prayers and praise by turns
  Cannot avail above.

Who, faultless, loveth Thee,
  Who lovingly believes
And penitently grieves,
  Shall reach supreme mukti.

GOOD WIVES.

How neat is the house of a virtuous wife!
  She shineth as light in a darkened recess.
The house that is ruled by a first-wedded wife
  Reminds of the house of our God.*

When love hath preceded the great wedding feast,
  The pair shall increase and shall spread as a tree,
Shall blossom and bud, shall rejoice in their strength,
  Producing abundance of fruit.

For riches are not the true wealth of a house.
  The first of all joys is the birth of a son.
But living together from youth to old age
  Is greatest of riches on earth.

If she should delight in her husband's desires,
  And both are united in heart and in mind,
Perfection they reach. For the wedded estate
  Leads on to our union with God.

* The first-wedded wife is the agent that ensures a happy home. While mutual love binds her and her husband, all goes well. When other wives are introduced, the first wife knows she has lost her husband's regard. Hence she neglects the house, is jealous of her lord, and shrewish to the new-comers. Then nothing goes well.

The Vedas are harlots, deluding our souls,
And who can discover the meaning they bear?
The knowledge of God, when the hidden is seen,
Is good as a true-hearted wife.

If she should compel the true love of her lord,
Then sweetest of happiness rests on their life.
But if she repel, then your happiness is—
Get rid of your wife when you can.

She who, in the time of her husband's life,
Should strive for the house, shall be loved by her sons.
In ups and in downs, as they come to us all,
The strength of strong sons is the best.

What sweeter than life can there be? Heaps of gold
Are better than thousands of other folks' lives.
What sweeter than gold? Loving words of a lass,
Whose love is the sweetest of all.

Far sweeter than sugar, than honey or cream,
And sweeter than juice of the sugar's long cane,
The heart of the Jack, or the Guava's ripe fruit,
Are words from the lips that we love.

To gaze on the face of a beauteous wife,—
To look at our sons in the pride of their strength,—
Are fuel to love. How they swell in the heart!
How easy to love them too much!

BAD WIVES.

Wives who disobey their lords
Are as death, as poison snakes;
Very demons. Yea, they are
Only fit to plague old Nick.

If they're thoughtless, they're no good;
Dowry is but thrown away.
Coward soldiers who would feed?
Why maintain a thoughtless quean?

See her wrangling in the street,
Screaming if you check her speech.
Scolds her lord and then she cries:
She would sell him in a bag.

Like the course of ships at sea,—
Like the flight of birds in air,—
Is a woman's life on earth.
Where she goes is never known.

Wealth is his,—the wife is good.
Wealth is gone—she loves no more:
Then her lord is but a name:
Then she counts him as the dead.

Wives who live to please their lords,
Wives indeed, the best on earth.
Wives who care for nought but self,
Are but arrows sent from death.

Low by nature, low in life:
Wife of worth you cannot make.
She who lives by stealing scraps
Cannot hope for better things.

Stubborn folks are always wrong.
Can you straighten puppy's tail?
Shrewish wives would sell their lords,—
Tie together hands and feet.

If you work and slave and gain,
Then your wife applauds your love.
Lose it all, and then she scolds,
Daily heaps reproach on you.

Though her lord and home be good
Will the changeful wife be true?
Though you rear a dog with milk
Will he learn to stay at home?

Suffering ills, look well to friends.
Fearing danger, watch your guards.
When your riches fly away,
Let your wife be closely watched.

If at first you fail to rule,
  Do not think to rule at all.
If you let a tree grow up,
  Will it move for but a push?

Disobedient wives are not
  Wives at all, but only gyves.
Better dwell in desert wastes
  Than abide with such a wife.

The preceding songs more than suffice to show that the relation of husband and wife is pretty nearly the same all the world over. While physical force is on the side of the men, the women will more than make themselves equal by power of the tongue. But both good and bad wives prove that the complete subordination of the wife, as laid down by Manu and everywhere preached, is only one of those theories that seem very excellent except in practice. As a matter of fact the Hindu wife that has escaped from the rigorous rule of her mother-in-law, and especially if she be a mother-in-law herself, is by far the most potential personage in the household. The husband seldom interferes in domestic matters, and sits on the pyall outside the house while the wife is busy with domestic duties within. We turn from these pleasant household scenes to a terrific onslaught upon the Brahmans.

BRAHMANS.

They who were Sudras born,
  And yet revile their kin;—
Who call themselves twice-born,
  And think it makes them safe;—
Whose hearts love darling sin;—
  The lowest Sudras are.*

Upon his brazen brow†
  He bears a sacred mark:
He has a wolfish mouth,
  A demon's shameless heart:
And yet he dares to say
  He knows the only God.

* The second birth of the Brahman does not take place until the thirteenth year, when the thread is first placed on his shoulders. Up to that period he is once-born, that is, is a Sudra. Vemana frequently refers to this fact and taunts the Brahmans with having been Sudras themselves. See for example the verse on the next page regarding the sacred thread.

† It is imperative on the twice-born to carry on their foreheads the mark of their god. The Vaishnavas wear a trident, the centre prong of which is continued just on to the bridge of the nose. The Saiva mark is a colored spot just above the nose. In addition to this the Saiva devotee should make three horizontal parallel lines with sandal-wood ash, extending from one temple to the other. A zealous worshipper of either Vishnu or Siva will carry the marks on his breast, arms and back.

He has an outcast's heart,*
And yet the outcaste scorns.
Shall he become twice-born,
Renewed in life and caste,
While no good thought exists
Within his sinful mind ?

The greatest sin of all
Is want of sterling truth.
But lie upon a lie
Is always in his mouth.
What rogues some Brahmans are,—
They call themselves twice-born!

They say, the lords of earth,
"How pure we are, how learned
In all the Shasters teach!"
They scorn us simple men!
But yet the poorest poor
Are better than such brags.

The Brahman thinks that when
He takes the sacred thread
His Sudraship is o'er.
How strangely he forgets
That when he comes to die
His Brahmanship is o'er.†

* Till the ceremony of the putting on of the thread the postulant is not a Brahman. He is not a member of any other caste and is, therefore, an out-caste.

† He cannot take his thread with him,—his new birth has failed him, for the dead are ceremonially unclean. If, therefore, he is not born a Brahman and cannot continue holy at death, what good is Brahmanship at all ?

And then he takes the dress
Of Somayaji state!*
And why? He's killed a goat,
Then cooked and ate it up!
He has the Brahman's name,
But where's the good result?

Just see how such men walk!
It shows they cannot know
The hidden things of God:
Their minds are far too light.
'Tis plain they know the way
To Yama's deepest hell.

They paint themselves with ash,
But this takes not away
The smell of drafts of wine.
Will strings around their neck
Convert such sinful men,
And render them twice-born?

If he should e'en forget
That he is flesh and blood,
And be so basely proud
That he is called twice-born,
Will fear seize death and hell?
Will they forsake their prey?

* This trenchant verse refers to the Yagnya sacrifice. At this ceremony a goat is roasted and every Brahman who assists in the rite is obliged to eat of the flesh. (Brown). This and other verses expressing horror at the thought of killing an animal would lead to the idea that Vemana was a Jain.

You foul your skin with ash:
What good will that do you?
Your thoughts should soar above:
Be set on God alone.
An ass can roll in mud
As well as any priest.

Bald head and matted locks!
Strange dress and mantras loud!
Outlandish cramps and pains
And all the ashy filth!
Ah! Bah! No man is good
Who is not pure in heart.

He leaves his house and wife,
With iron binds his loins,
Prefers bad food to good,
And bitter drink to sweet!
Will living like a beast
Secure him endless bliss?*

* These are some of the verses that express Vemana's dislike of a yogi's life. If written by him, and they tally with much that must be ascribed to his hand, it would be incredible that Vemana was a yogi or jangam. It appears to me that the many expressions praising the jangams have been added by one of the many revisors or collectors whose handiwork is so visible throughout the series. The last verse but one describes the habits of the yogi or sanyassi. They must be familiar to all readers of Indian literature, although few will have deemed it possible for a Hindu to speak so frankly of their utter folly and vanity. English rule and western ideas are now making sad inroads on the yogi's profits.

POOR RICHARD.

Do nothing slowly, else 'twill never come to pass:
Do nothing hurriedly, for then 'twill surely fail.
Will unripe fruit grow ripe if cut too soon?

In water ships ride easily: yet on the land
Cannot be moved a step. And thus the skilful man
Is only worth his salt at his own trade.

The crocodile will kill an elephant within its stream,
And yet on land a little dog can master it.
Thus things are strong when in their proper place.

A pig will have at least a dozen little ones:
The giant lordly elephant can have but one.
Is not one worthy man enough at once?

What teacher fails to benefit the clever man?
What man, however wise, can teach a stupid fool?
For who can make a crooked river straight?

The empty man will always talk in boastful style:
The excellent will keep his peace or gently speak.
Will gold ring out, when struck, like brazen bells?

The mighty Ganges flows in peace, with quiet stream :
But with a roar leaps down the short-lived turbid brook.
The base are not as quiet as the good.

To kill a miser needs no deadly poisoned draft.
Just try this method. Ask him for a gift of pice,*
And he will instantly fall down and die.

He who will neither eat nor let his friends partake,
Is but a vicious wretch. Just like the grinning face
Set up to scare the birds from ripening corn.†

Behold the swelling fig. Outside 'tis like pure gold;
But bite it, then you find it holds but worms.
How like the silence of the empty man!

The man who gives the rein to all his passions vile
Is mad as any hare. He wanders o'er the earth.
Desiring wrongful gain, he doubles like a dog.

Will those who love a lie e'er prosper like the good?
Will fortune smile on them or glorify their home?
'Tis drawing water with a leaky pot.

* Eight pice make one penny, and the pice is therefore worth just half a farthing. It is the smallest copper coin in the world perhaps, certainly the smallest in the British empire.

† Here we have the Dravidian representative of the "dog in the manger," both in its image and its moral. The scare-crow has to serve a double purpose, guarding the corn from the birds and from the "evil-eye" of men.

DOMESTIC MORALITY.

They that leave the wife at home,
  After prostitutes to roam,
Are but mad. They leave good crops
  For the straw the gleaner drops.

Thieves and harlots love the night,
  Ever hiding from the light.
Neither dare to see the moon
  Rising o'er the dark night's gloom.

Never sport with these four things,
  Either one destruction brings—
Fire, and weapons made to kill,
  Princes, women given to ill.

Wrongful speech we may set right:
  Stones be cut by any wight:
But the mind no man can mend,
  As it was, 'tis to the end.

If but wisdom fill his mouth
  What concerns his age or youth?
Will the lamp become less bright
  If an infant hold its light?

Pour the water on the seed,—
  Soon it sprouts, then leaves succeed.
Next the buds to flowers blow,
  And a tree on earth doth grow.

Talk is easy, virtue hard:
  We may teach, yet not regard:
Any fool a sword can hold,
  None can wield it but the bold.

Writ in water what will stay?
  So our blessings fade away.
Foolish man for surety longs,
  Trusts to words to right his wrongs.

When misfortune comes to be,
  He reviles the deity.
Lauds himself when good things come.
  Good and ill are both our own.

If your fault offend your lord,
  Do not blame his angry word:
Else you'd count among your foes
  Glass that shows your crooked nose.

Riches, like a woman's charms,
  Fly away like ghostly forms;
As the moonlight's glory fades
  When a cloud its crescent shades.

PROVERBS.

Wealth he heaps, gives none away,
Useth none, in earth doth lay.
Knows, he not how men devour
What the bee hides in his bower ?*

You may break a granite stone:
Highest hills may crumble down:
But a hardened cruel screw
Naught will soften or subdue.

Misers cannot see, and live,
Liberal men their wealth to give.
Like the thorn that always dies
Near the tree of Paradise.†

Milk that's drunk at tavern door
Counts as wine, you may be sure.
If you stand where you ought not
Why be shocked when shame is got.

* There are many passages in Vemana like this, showing that, as in Russia tyranny is kept within bounds by fear of assassination, so wealth under native rulers in India was kept down by the certainty of confiscation, if the Rajah or Nabob got scent of it. No man can perfectly hide rapidly growing wealth.

† Compare the second verse on Page 291. The miser is a favorite butt of the Hindoo poet.

Join the vile, and vile you'll be
  In the eyes of those who see.
If beneath a palm you drink,*
  Though but milk, what must we think?

Blind man's legs the lame man plies,
  Cripples lend the blind their eyes:
Thus for each the poor take heed,
  Help each other's urgent need.†

Give promotion to the rude,
  They will chase away the good.
Can the dog that eats old shoes
  Taste the sugarcane he chews?

Wash a bear skin every day,
  Will its blackness go away?‡
If you beat an idol's face
  Will the god acquire new grace?

* All the fermented liquors used in Southern India are made from the juices of the Palmyra and Cocoanut palms. When the juice is freshly drawn it is called "toddy," and even then is somewhat intoxicating. If a man drink beneath a palm-tree we are justified in thinking his beverage is toddy, for we judge a man by the company he keeps.

† This anticipates the English fable of the blind and lame beggars—the latter guided, the former trudged, and both flourished.

‡ How often do these epigrams bring to mind the parallel passages that abound in European literature and folk-lore! Among the Dravidian middle classes, proverbs and epigrams form a large proportion of all conversation. While a European, who does not catch the idiom, stands dumb with astonishment at the nonsense his native hosts or friends utter, they are in reality making the most trenchant repartees, putting in single neat sentences arguments which would cover a page if expressed in any other form.

FINAL PHILOSOPHY.

If you swim, you fear no stream.
  Poverty is but a dream
When a girdle makes you rich.
  Waiting death, earth has no hitch.

Catch a monkey, dress it well,
  'Tis the king of all the hill.
Thus, 'mongst men, the senseless rule,
  And the luckless serve the fool.

Snakes are finest when they strike:
  Deadly foes your friendship like:
When the king would take your head,
  Perfect freedom leaves you dead.

Water dropped in oyster shell
  Brought forth pearls. But that which fell
On the sea is water still.*
  Wrongful time turns good to ill.

If a fool should find the stone†
  It would not remain his own.
It would melt, escape again,
  Like the hail that comes with rain.

* Is it possible to account for this constant repetition of Aryan ideas except on the supposition of a common origin?

† The philosopher's stone—as great an object of search in India now as in Europe during the middle ages.

INDEX.